# Rice, Spice and all Things Nice

# Rice, Spice and all Things Nice

## REZA MAHAMMAD

SIMON & SCHUSTER
A CBS COMPANY

**Author's acknowledgements:** Chef Brinder Narula from The Star of India for his expertise and seemingly boundless knowledge! Capel and Land, my agents, for their encouragement and enthusiasm. Thank you to my friends too numerous to mention, who have tried to keep me grounded and for controlling my flights of fancy. You know who you are.

**Special thanks:** Robin Seymour of The Refinery (Films) for generously contributing his unique photographic ability. Rahil Chaudhari for his invaluable support and guidance. Special thanks to my harem of invaluable and talented women: Rena Valeh, for her brilliant brain without whose help I could not have accomplished this book; Zelie Hilton, who has been an effective field-marshal throughout this project, and my sister, Farah Kadiri, who spent countless hours trying out recipes and allowed me to invade her kitchen.

First published in Great Britain by Simon & Schuster UK Ltd. 2006
A CBS Company
This paperback edition first published 2007
Copyright © Simon and Schuster

Simon & Schuster UK Ltd
Africa House, 64-78 Kingsway, London, WC2B 6AH

Design: Jane Humphrey
Food photography: Steve Lee
Styling: Liz Belton
Home economy: Harry Eastwood

Printed and bound in China

ISBN 9781847370495

Photo credits: Pages 6, 12, 17, 18, 35, 38, 41, 42, 52, 69, 74, 99, 100, 118, 121, 150, 175 copyright © Robin Seymour; Pages 50-51, 54-55, 58-59, 64-65, 88, 92, 96, 134-135, 141, 153 copyright © Janice Broxup - Shooting Star Television; Pages 45, 80-81, 115, 116, 164 copyright © Tiger Aspect Productions

# CONTENTS

Cooking is the new rock 'n' roll, which is lucky, as last week it was gardening, or was it property? The irony is, of course, that for many people nowadays — some of my friends included — cooking means 'remove packaging, pierce film lid and place in microwave for 3 minutes'. If you're one of those people, what on earth were you doing in the cookery section of the bookshop in the first place?

If you are a serial microwaver, this is the book to inspire you to use that thing in the kitchen with the trap door and rings, otherwise known as a cooker. And you'll be amazed at what you can create. And guess what? You'll enjoy it, I promise. If you're already a kitchen diva, then you'll find recipes that will allow you to display your culinary skills and experiment with dishes you may not be familiar with.

Are you sitting comfortably? What would you like to know first, me or the recipes? OK, don't all shout at once. It's me then, so we can dispense with the 'me' factor. I went to boarding school in India — the same one as Freddie Mercury since you ask. He was fascinated by my culinary expertise. Well, I'm sure he would have been had we been there at the same time. But it is one of my fantasies, so indulge me. In fact, we never met, much to his chagrin, I'm sure. I spent my holidays in the Western Ghats with my aunts and uncles. While my cousins were climbing trees and playing cricket, I disappeared to the kitchen, spellbound by the exotic aromas, captivated by the chopping of herbs, grinding of spices on stone, extracting of coconut milk for rice dishes, the cauldrons in the burning embers and the pickles, jams and preserves. It was a different world, and one that I found endlessly fascinating. It was hypnotic – the extraordinary alchemy of ingredients and flavours. And from then on I was hooked. I still am.

This love affair is surely in the genes. My father came to the UK in 1937 and after working in Veeraswamy became known as one of the pioneers of Indian cookery in Britain with the establishment of the Star of India. I, however, never really thought of my father as a chef; to me he was simply a successful businessman who left the house each day for the office (which happened to be a restaurant). My mother knew better: the kitchen at home was very much her domain, but she would always consult my father about the dishes she prepared.

The recipes in this book are mostly the result of my travels and filming, though some come from the Star of India and others are family recipes. Some are so simple you'll be able to pick them up very quickly. Others require rather more time and effort, but are worth it, especially if you're having a dinner party. You really will impress your friends. And before you know it, you'll be roasting and grinding your own spices with a flourish you never knew you possessed. And if you're not that way inclined, the supermarket ready-ground ones will do nicely. What I have tried to provide in this book is a flavour and taste of India and, above all, to share the joy and excitement of preparing Indian food. The basics are crucial and the do-it-yourself aspect of preparing a dish from scratch makes it fun as well as delicious.

Any recipe becomes your recipe. We've all met those infuriating people who make wonderful food, then, when you ask for the recipe, say they can't tell you because they never measure anything. When you're writing a recipe book, you don't have that luxury. But I think it's important to remember that any recipe is really only a guideline. It gives you a foundation from which to work. If you find a recipe that appeals to you, but contains an ingredient you can't bear, or not enough of one that you love, don't be put off. Play around with it and experiment. Feel free to make your own version. But remember – if it turns out better than the recipe I've given you, just promise you won't tell my publisher/agent.

Aside from cooking, my other love is music and I have come to realise that the two are linked because Indian food is like music: a symphony of taste. Each dish has its own intricate beats and rhythm, like the strumming of a sitar, as the flavours hit the palate. *Enjoy!*

# Reza's rules

**Read these before you even touch a pan unless you need to use it as a weapon.**

**1**  be prepared

Make sure all your ingredients are measured and lined up, in the order in which you will need them, before you start to cook. Often, though the list of ingredients looks dauntingly long, the method of cooking is quite simple. If you find you are missing one or two spices from a long list, don't be put off, you can still make the dish. More on this in Rule 2.

**2**  jazz it up

Variety is the spice of life, and you will find plenty of spices in these recipes. It's important, though, to treat spices with respect. In particular, follow these guidelines:

Try to buy whole spices, as they keep longer than ground ones. If you can only buy ground spices, store them in airtight containers away from sunlight in order to prolong their life.

To get maximum flavour from your whole spices, first roast them in a dry pan for a few minutes until they become aromatic, then grind them.

Don't despair if you haven't got all the spices listed in a recipe. Improvise, that way it'll be your own version. If the name of a spice is in the title of the recipe – as in Lamb with Fenugreek or Lamb with Pickling Spices – it's obviously essential.

**3**  go easy on yourself

Help is at hand – use it. The recipes in each section are in order of increasing difficulty; in other words the easier recipes are at the start of each chapter. If you are a keen Indian food fan, it is worth your while investing in the following pieces of equipment, all of which will make your life much easier but won't break the bank:

*Microplane*  This is ideal for grating garlic and ginger. If you have one, ignore recipe instructions that say crush or finely chop these ingredients, just grate them.

*Wet and dry grinder* Lakeland do one which both grinds dry spices and makes pastes with wetter ingredients. Braun has a 'multi-trio' that will produce small quantities of purées and pastes, though it doesn't double as a spice grinder. Both will cope with small quantities much better than a food processor or blender. You can also get good results with a pestle and mortar, and, though the paste will be coarser, it will work fine.

*Heat diffuser* This is essential if you want to achieve the minimum heat necessary for long slow cooking and steaming rice. It's especially useful for biryanis where you don't want the rice to catch on the bottom of the pan.

*Flat griddle* Great for making breads, chapatis and parathas, but your good old frying pan will do.

## 4 be brave

Don't be put off by unfamiliar terms such as 'tempering', which is used in almost all the recipes. This merely involves heating oil until it is very hot, adding whole spices to release their oils, and then adding them to the dish at the required time. Mustard seeds need to crackle and pop in the hot oil or they will be indigestible.

Don't be afraid of trying these dishes out on your friends. Something like Haleem (page 104) or the Spiced Whole Leg of Lamb (page 90) would make a great alternative Sunday lunch; you can always go easy on the chillies if you are not sure of your audience.

**a note on numbers** Where a recipe says 'Serves 4–6, etc', it will be enough for the higher number if you are making more than one main dish with accompaniments. Otherwise, it will serve the lower number with rice and/or a vegetable.

# notes on ingredients

All these ingredients are readily available in Indian food shops. Some can also be found in Thai and Middle Eastern shops. Where possible, I've given alternatives for the more unusual items.

**asafoetida** *(Hing)*

This is an anti-flatulent and therefore is added to many bean and lentil dishes to aid digestion. It is always added to the hot oil before any other ingredients. It's also known as Devil's dung because of its pungent pong.

**black cumin** see cumin

**breadcrumbs**

If you have no stale bread for your crumbs, put a few slices of fresh bread into a low oven for 10 minutes or so to dry out. You can use any bread. This way, they will whizz into crumbs rather than a greyish paste.

**cardamom** *(Elaichi)*

Cardamom is known as the queen of spices. There are two kinds: black and green. The black is used mainly for garam masala and rice dishes. Use whole pods for these. The more common variety is the green cardamom which can be used, either whole or ground, in sweet and savoury dishes. If a recipe just says cardamom, use the green kind.

**chaat masala**

This consists of black salt, dry mango, musk melon, cumin, black pepper, pomegranate seeds, coriander, mint, dried ginger, nutmeg, chillies, caraway, cloves and asafoetida. Don't worry, I'm not expecting you to make it yourself, I just thought you'd like to know what goes into it. Just buy it ready-made.

**chana masala**

This is made up of salt, coriander, dry mango, pomegranate, chillies, cumin, musk melon, black pepper, black salt, fenugreek seeds, cloves, mint, nutmeg, dried ginger, cinnamon, bay leaf, caraway and mace. In other words, everything but the kitchen sink. Again, I don't expect you to make it yourself. This can be bought in most Asian corner shops.

**chapati flour** *(Ata)*

Very finely ground wholewheat flour. If you can't find it, substitute wheatmeal flour. Failing that, use wholemeal but sift it first through a fine sieve to remove some of the bran.

**charoli**

Also known as chironji or cudpahnut. Try to find them if at all possible, as they have a very special flavour. Don't worry, there's only one recipe where you'll need them.

### chillies

Unlike most things in life, with chillies smaller is stronger. We tend to use the long, thin, green chillies that are about 2–3 inches long, but you can use any variety that suits you. Unless otherwise specified, de-seed for a mild dish or keep the seeds in for a bit more of a kick.

### coconut *(Narial)*

I have used several variations on a theme of these brown hairy fruits: coconut milk is now so widely available in supermarkets that it's hardly worth mentioning that you can make it from the fresh fruit or from coconut powder.

Fresh grated coconut can be found frozen in most Thai specialist shops. Unsweetened desiccated coconut, soaked in warm water for 10–20 minutes and squeezed dry, will work in any of the recipes using fresh coconut. You will need half the weight of fresh coconut. You can also toast desiccated coconut if fresh is unavailable, for example in the Beef Coconut Fry (page 89). I've included this in the Keralan recipes for authenticity and the fact that coconut oil is probably responsible for the glossy hair and glowing skins of the South Indians. However, if you're already thinning on top and the wrinkles are showing, forget it. It is also very high in cholesterol so vegetable oil is a healthier option.

### coriander *(Dhania)*

Both the leaf and seeds of coriander are essential ingredients in Indian cooking. The leaf is the equivalent of parsley in English cooking. The seeds, which are one of the main ingredients of commercial curry powder, are best bought whole and roasted and ground as required.

### cumin *(Jeera)*

Used whole in hot oil for tempering, it is another spice that's best bought whole and roasted and ground as and when required. Black cumin is more potent than the usual cumin. I've only used it in one of the biryani dishes. If it's difficult to find, just use ordinary cumin.

### curry leaves

These small, almond-shaped leaves with a citrus taste are commonly used for tempering. They can be bought fresh or dried. However, I recommend you buy them fresh and freeze them for future use. You can use them straight from the freezer and they keep for ages.

### dal see lentils

### fennel seeds *(Saunf)*

Fennel seeds are a much-loved spice used throughout India. They are used either whole or in powdered form. They are easier to grind if you roast them first. The aniseed flavour is great as a mouth freshener and is also said to help alleviate wind and aid digestion. Did you know that the Roman Army marched for miles due to their high consumption of fennel?

### fenugreek *(Methi)*

Fenugreek has a bitter and strong flavour. I've used both fresh and dried leaves, as well as seeds, in this book. The fresh leaves are not as pungent in taste as the dried leaves and don't have as strong an aroma. The dried leaves, known as kasturi methi, are generally added at the end of cooking and can alter and enhance the flavour of the dish. They should only be used sparingly, so follow the quantity guide accurately. The seeds are used for pickling and tempering.

In the recipe for Methi Paratha (page 43), you could use spinach instead of the fresh fenugreek and add a teaspoon of either the dried leaves or ground seeds.

### garlic

If you're going to do a lot of Indian cooking, you may want to make up a quantity of garlic paste to save time. It will keep for a week in the refrigerator, or two weeks if you substitute oil for the water. It also freezes well. Blend peeled garlic cloves with half a teaspoon of salt and just enough water to make a paste in a food processor or blender. You will need enough garlic for the blades to chop efficiently. About 200 g (7 oz) should do.

### garam masala

Although the term means hot spices, it is actually a combination of several spices which have been dry roasted and then ground into a fine powder. It has a lovely, rich, warm aroma and is added to many of my recipes. Everyone has their own recipe for garam masala; the one that appears below is the one we use at the Star of India. If you don't have the time to make it, you can buy ready-made garam masala almost everywhere.

| | | | |
|---:|---|---:|---|
| 8 | **bay leaves** | 1 tbsp | **cloves** |
| 6–8 5 cm (2 inch) | **sticks cinnamon** | 2 tbsp | **green cardamoms** |
| 50 g (2 oz) | **coriander seeds** | 4–6 | **whole black cardamoms** |
| 50 g (2 oz) | **cumin seeds** | 4–6 | **star anise** |
| 1 tbsp | **fennel seeds** | 8–10 | **blades mace** |
| 1 tbsp | **black peppercorns** | 1–2 tbsp | **dried pink rose petals** |

Dry roast all the ingredients in a wide-based non-stick pan for 5–7 minutes, then allow to cool. Grind in a coffee mill until a very fine powder. Store in an airtight container in a cool, dark place.

### ghee

Ghee is clarified butter and is rich in texture but will not totally solidify. It can be heated to a very high temperature without burning and does not need to be refrigerated. However, if your ghee-pot is empty, a mixture of butter and oil, which will stop the butter burning, should do the trick.

### ginger

As with garlic, if you intend to make several dishes using grated ginger, you may find it more efficient to make up a quantity of ginger paste in advance rather than grating small amounts for each recipe. Follow the instructions under 'Garlic' using ginger instead, though it isn't necessary to use oil.

### gram flour

This is chickpea flour, which is generally used for making pakoras and as a thickening agent in soups and sauces. Although it is commonly available, you could substitute plain flour if necessary.

### green mango

The green refers not to the colour of the skin but to their lack of ripeness. It is best to buy these in Indian or Thai shops, which sell the right varieties for use as cooking mangoes.

### green papaya

These are unripe papayas, and can often be found in Thai shops, as well as Indian grocers. In the Hyderabadi Spring Lamb Biryani recipe (page 156), the papaya is used as a tenderiser. If you can't find it, use the same quantity of pineapple juice in the marinade. Unfortunately, there is no substitute for it in the recipe for Spicy Papaya Salad (page 131).

### jaggery

This is unrefined sugar from the sugar-cane, sticky and sweet. You can use palm sugar or light muscovado as substitutes.

### khoa

This is concentrated, dried milk. It comes in blocks, which can be grated. If necessary, you can use the equivalent amount of dried milk. It adds richness to sauces, but can be omitted.

### kokum

Also known as black mangosteen, these small, sour berries can be bought dried. Soak them to soften them before use. Tamarind is a perfect substitute. Failing that, use either lemon or lime juice.

### lentils

*Toor* are oiled yellow split peas, smaller than chana dal, used mostly in South Indian cooking.
*Black masoor* are very similar to Puy lentils, which can be used as a substitute.
*Urad* come in both black and white forms, both of which are used in this book. See note under chana about tempering.
*Chana* are similar to yellow split peas, but are slightly smaller and meatier. Yellow split peas can be used as a substitute. When tempering urad and chana lentils, use the white urad lentil and the yellow split peas. Wherever these ingredients are specified for tempering, they are optional. Use them if you have them, but the recipe will be fine without them.
*Masoor* are red split lentils, the most common kind and they turn yellow when cooked.
*Moong/Mung* are small, yellow split lentils (the ones used for bean sprouts).

**mustard oil**

A strong-flavoured viscous oil. If you prefer a lighter flavour, substitute vegetable oil.

**mustard seeds**

There are yellow and black varieties of mustard seed. It is the black ones that are used in this book.

**oils**

Any vegetable oil can be used except olive oil.

**onions** *fried*

Wherever the method says 'fry the onions till golden brown', this means quite brown in European cooking terms. They need to take on a rich colour. Fried onions for garnish are deep brown and crisp, without being burnt. For large quantities, deep frying is quickest, but you can shallow fry smaller amounts over a medium-to-high heat, with enough oil to liberally cover the base of your frying pan. They store well in airtight containers when well drained and cold.

**paneer**

Home-made cottage cheese, which is available in blocks. You can easily make your own by following the recipe below. In the Saag Paneer recipe (page 110), I've used the bought variety, which is harder, and therefore easier to grate. If you make your own it will be too soft to grate, so just crumble it into the spinach. Bring 1.7 litres (3 pints) of milk to the boil. As soon as it rises, remove from the heat and add lemon juice, a teaspoonful at a time, until the milk curdles. The curd will separate from the whey. Do not add more lemon juice than necessary as this will harden the paneer. Drain through a sieve lined with muslin or a clean J-cloth. Squeeze out as much liquid as possible and leave in the cloth to drain while it cools.

**poppy seeds** *(Khus khus)*

It is the white variety that is used in Indian cookery, unlike the black ones used in European cooking.

**saffron**

I tend to use strands, soaked in water or milk depending on the recipe, but powdered will do fine.

**samosa pastry**

Also known as samosa pads, these are found only in Indian shops. But we can give the Chinese a look-in: use spring-roll wrappers instead.

**tamarind**

Translates as 'the date of India' – interpret as you will. Used as a souring agent, it's found fresh or dried in blocks or as a concentrate (paste). You can use any one of these, or failing that, lemon or lime juice. For the Tamarind Chutney (page 138), try to get the fresh (wet) block which has seeds in it, though the dried version will do just as well.

One of the memories of India that visitors always carry with them is the street food stalls. Sometimes the memories aren't always pleasant, because if you're unaccustomed to street food, it can have an adverse effect on your stomach! **We love grazing**, so the following dishes can be eaten as snacks, starters or light supper dishes. Samosas and pakoras are a great favourite. They're often served at teatime in Asian homes, much like tea and cakes in Britain.

I've also included various breads in this section, because they tend to be eaten as snacks; some have fillings and others, like chapatis, can be eaten on their own or as accompaniments to main dishes.

# SOUPS, SNACKS AND BREADS

# Indian-style scrambled eggs *(Khagina)*

An Indian slant to an old favourite. This is a really homely dish, suitable for breakfast, a light lunch, or when you return tired after a hard day's night. I particularly love it with garlic, as it brings out the flavour of the eggs, but you might not want to include it for breakfast!

| | |
|---:|:---|
| 8 | **eggs** *beaten* |
| 1 ¹/₂ tbsp | **ghee** |
| 1 medium | **onion** *finely chopped* |
| 5 | **cloves** |
| 2 x 5 cm (2 inch) | **cinnamon sticks** |
| 5 | **cardamom pods** |
| 1 | **garlic clove** *crushed (optional)* |
| 1–2 | **green chillies** *finely chopped* |
| ¹/₄ tsp | **ground turmeric** |
| 1 | **tomato** *diced* |
| | **salt and freshly ground black pepper** |
| 1 tbsp | **coriander** *freshly chopped* |

**serves 4–6**   Heat the ghee in a non-stick pan, then add the onion, plus a pinch of salt to help bring out its sweetness, and sauté until translucent. Add the cloves, cinnamon, cardamom, garlic and chillies. Stir in the turmeric, and continue to cook on a low heat for a further 3–4 minutes, to allow the onion to soften.

Add the tomato and salt lightly. Reduce the mixture until soft and mushy. Add the eggs, black pepper and coriander. Mix gently, allowing the eggs to form clusters, but make sure you do not overcook them. Remove from the heat and serve immediately.

# pepper soup *(Rasam)*

This warming, South Indian soup is one of the best ways to ward off a cold and keep those chills at bay. It contains all the healing properties you need when you are feeling poorly, and helps line the stomach and aid digestion. It can be accompanied with plain rice or eaten on its own. Health conscious South Indians make a light meal of this easily digestible rasam. The tamarind, tomatoes and lime give it a piquant, tangy taste.

| | |
|---|---|
| 3 | **garlic cloves** |
| 1 tsp | **cumin seeds** |
| $^1/_2$ tsp | **ground turmeric** |
| 1 tsp | **black peppercorns** |
| 3 tbsp | **coconut oil or vegetable oil** |
| pinch | **asafoetida** |
| 1 tsp | **black mustard seeds** |
| 2 sprigs | **curry leaves** *(16–20 leaves)* |
| 1 small | **green mango** *peeled and finely diced (see notes on ingredients)* |
| 2 tsp | **tamarind paste** |
| 2 | **tomatoes** *chopped* |
| 3 tbsp | **coriander** *freshly chopped* |

**serves 4**   Grind or pound the garlic, cumin seeds, turmeric and peppercorns to a smooth paste, along with a dash of water. You can do this either in a small blender or using a pestle and mortar.

Heat the coconut oil in a saucepan and add the asafoetida, mustard seeds and curry leaves. Stir and fry for a few seconds, then add the spice paste. Reduce the heat to low and fry the paste for 1–2 minutes. Tip in the mango and pour in 700 ml ($1^1/_4$ pints) water.

Bring the soup to a simmer and cook for about 5 minutes. Just before serving, stir in the tamarind paste, tomatoes and coriander. Serve either on its own, or with a mound of fluffy rice.

# chicken kofta and rice broth

Just as every Jewish mamma has her own version of chicken soup, so every Muslim mamma has her own take on this nourishing dish.

The use of dill comes from Persian/Afghani influences while the spices give it an Indian twist. The koftas are highly seasoned, which gives a warming sensation to the chest. A light and delicate broth, this becomes, with the addition of rice and carrots, a meal in itself.

| | for the chicken kofta | | for the broth |
|---|---|---|---|
| 300 g (10 oz) | **chicken breast** *skinned* | 50 g (2 oz) | **butter** |
| 3 | **garlic cloves** *coarsely chopped* | 1 medium | **carrot** *cut into julienne strips* |
| 5 cm (2 inch) piece | **fresh ginger** *coarsely chopped* | 1 | **clove garlic** *crushed to a fine paste with a* |
| 1 small bunch | **fresh coriander** *roughly chopped* | | *dash of salt* |
| 1 small bunch | **dill** *roughly chopped* | 3 x 2.5 cm (1 inch) | **cinnamon sticks** |
| 1–2 | **green chillies** *chopped* | 3 | **cardamom pods** |
| 1 tsp | **garam masala** | 5 | **black peppercorns** |
| | **salt** | 3 | **bay leaves** |
| | | 60 g (2¼ oz) | **basmati rice** *washed and left to soak for* |
| | | | *30 minutes* |
| | | 1 | **tomato** *de-seeded, diced and lightly salted* |

**serves 4**   Place the chicken in a food processor, along with the garlic, ginger, green chillies, garam masala and salt, to taste, together with the coriander and dill, leaving approximately 1 tbsp of each of the herbs for garnish. Process to a fine mince, combining all the ingredients thoroughly. Shape the mixture into balls into koftas the size of a ping-pong ball and set aside.

Melt the butter in a large saucepan. Add the garlic and carrot and allow them to sweat for a couple of minutes before adding the cinnamon, cardamom, peppercorns and bay leaves. Pour on 500 ml (18 fl oz) water and bring to the boil. Gently place the kofta balls in the liquid, lower the heat and simmer for approximately 5 minutes. Drain the rice and add it to the pan and continue to cook. When the rice and koftas are nearly ready, add the diced tomato and garnish with the remaining chopped dill and coriander.

# tomato soup

This is a light, refreshing summer soup. While it is a typically South Indian dish, I happened to come across this recipe at a market in Auckland, New Zealand, when I was doing my Christmas shopping. It was completely unexpected, so far from home, be it India or England.

Christmas shopping is such a chore that I decided to make things easier by hopping on a plane for a 24-hour flight. Maybe a rather radical way of avoiding the crowds on Oxford Street, but there's simply nowhere to park. Especially if you don't have a car.

| | |
|---|---|
| 10 | **ripe plum tomatoes** |
| | **salt** |
| | |
| | **for the spice powder** |
| $^1/_2$ tsp | **oil** |
| $^1/_2$ tsp | **urad lentils** |
| $^1/_2$ tsp | **chana lentils** |
| 1 tsp | **whole cumin seeds** |
| 1 tsp | **coriander seeds** |
| $^1/_4$ tsp | **fenugreek seeds** |

| | |
|---|---|
| | **for the tempering** |
| 1 tbsp | **vegetable oil** |
| $^1/_4$ tsp | **asafoetida** |
| 1 tsp | **mustard seeds** |
| 1 sprig | **curry leaves** *(8–10 leaves)* |
| 1 tbsp | **fresh coriander** *finely chopped* |

**serves 4** Place the tomatoes in a large saucepan, add 1 litre (1$^3/_4$ pints) water, bring to the boil and cook the tomatoes until they have broken down and become pulpy. Allow to cool completely.

Coat the base of a small frying pan with the oil and, when hot, add the urad and chana lentils and sauté. Add the cumin seeds, coriander seeds and fenugreek seeds and continue to fry until golden brown. Allow the mixture to cool, then either grind it to a fine powder in a coffee mill or pound it in a pestle and mortar. Pour this powder into a blender and add the cooled tomato. Blend together and then strain the liquid through a fine sieve to remove any sediment and skin. Return the strained liquid to the saucepan and heat through.

In a separate frying pan, heat the vegetable oil until hot, add the asafoetida and allow it to sizzle. Put in the mustard seeds, curry leaves and coriander and stir briskly for a couple of seconds. Tip this mixture into the soup, bring it to the boil, and add salt if necessary. Serve either hot or cold.

# lamb and herb soup

A wholesome soup, wonderful on a chilly winter's day. It has most of the vitamins that help ward off colds. Both adults and children will enjoy the subtle flavours on offer. We use leg of lamb and include the bone, which makes a rich stock. You may find it easier to use boneless, cubed lamb.

| | |
|---|---|
| 400 g (14 oz) | **lamb** cubed |
| pinch | **saffron strands** |
| 175 g (6 oz) | **canned chickpeas** drained and rinsed |
| 175 g (6 oz) | **canned pinto beans** drained and rinsed (optional) |
| | **salt and freshly ground black pepper** |

| | |
|---|---|
| | **for the bouquet garni** (tied together in a square of muslin for easy removal) |
| 1 small | **onion** coarsely chopped |
| 3–4 | **garlic cloves** quartered |
| 5 cm (2 inch) piece | **fresh ginger** cut into julienne strips |
| 1/2 tsp | **whole black peppercorns** |
| 10 | **whole cardamoms** |
| 6–8 | **cloves** |
| 4 x 5 cm (2 inch) | **cinnamon sticks** |

| | |
|---|---|
| | **for the garnish** |
| 1 tbsp | **fresh parsley** finely chopped |
| 115 g (4 oz) | **spring onions** finely chopped |
| 1 tbsp | **mint** finely chopped |
| 1 tsp | **dried lime powder or the juice of 1 lemon or 2 limes** |

**serves 6**  Put the meat in a wide casserole or large lidded pan, along with 2 litres ($3^1/2$ pints) water, and bring to the boil, removing any scum that comes to the surface. Reduce to simmer, add the bouquet garni and a few strands of saffron, then cover and cook gently on a medium-to-low heat for 2 hours until the meat is tender. Add the chickpeas and pinto beans and heat through. Just before serving, stir in the parsley, spring onions, mint and lime powder. Allow to cook for a further 5–10 minutes, then season with salt and pepper. Serve with warm bread.

# potato cakes *(Chowk Ki Tikki)*

This recipe has got such a great name, you'll want to make it simply so you have an excuse to say it. Chowk means street and tikki is a kind of cake or cutlet. So, guess what? This means street cake. It's a particularly good recipe for vegetarians and it's fab served with the spiced chickpeas.

Frozen peas work as well as shelled fresh peas, plus they cut down on preparation time. The potato cakes can also be prepared up to a day in advance and kept in the refrigerator until needed.

**for the potato cakes**

| | |
|---|---|
| 4 medium | **white or red potatoes** *boiled in their skins, peeled and then left to rest in the refrigerator for 24 hours* |
| 2 | **slices white bread** |
| 1 tsp | **chat masala** |
| 1 tsp | **chilli powder** |
| | **salt** |
| | **oil for frying** |

**for the stuffing**

| | |
|---|---|
| 1 tsp | **oil** |
| 1/2 tsp | **cumin seeds** |
| pinch | **asafoetida** |
| 1 cm (1/2 inch) piece | **fresh ginger** *peeled and finely grated or chopped* |
| 2 | **garlic cloves** *finely grated or chopped* |
| 1 | **green chilli** *de-seeded and slivered* |
| 100 g (3 1/2 oz) | **fresh or frozen peas** *cooked and drained* |

**for the spiced chick peas**

| | |
|---|---|
| 200 g (7 oz) | **chickpeas** *cooked and drained* |
| 1 tbsp | **oil** |
| 2.5 cm (1 inch) piece | **fresh ginger** *peeled and chopped* |
| 1 | **garlic clove** *crushed* |
| 1 tsp | **chana masala** |
| 1 tbsp | **tomato purée** |

**for the garnish**

| | |
|---|---|
| 3 tbsp | **natural yoghurt** |
| 1 tsp | **chana masala** |
| 1 tbsp | **fresh coriander** *chopped* |

**serves 6** Remove the crusts from the bread slices and make into breadcrumbs using a food processor. Remove the potatoes from the refrigerator and either grate them on the fine side of a grater, or mash them. Add the chat masala, chilli powder, a pinch of salt and the breadcrumbs, and knead together like dough. Divide the mixture into 12 equal portions and flatten into discs.

Next make the stuffing. Heat the oil in a frying pan and, when hot, add the cumin seeds. Allow them to sizzle, then add the asafoetida, ginger, garlic, chilli and some salt, stirring continuously for a few seconds. Add the peas and continue to fry until the mixture has become dry. Remove from the heat and allow to cool.

Place a spoonful of the stuffing mixture in the centre of each of the potato discs. Gather up the sides and shape into round cakes, smoothing out any cracks around the edges. Either deep fry or shallow fry the potato cakes in vegetable oil until golden. Remove with a slotted spoon and place on kitchen paper to drain off any excess oil.

To prepare the topping, heat the oil in a separate pan, then add the chickpeas, ginger, garlic, chana masala and tomato purée. Add a tablespoon of water to moisten and cook for 2–3 minutes until all the flavours have infused.

Serve hot in individual bowls, placing a couple of the fried tikkis in the centre. Add a tablespoon of the chickpea mixture and a dollop of yoghurt. Finally, garnish with a sprinkle of chana masala and chopped coriander.

# melt-in-the-mouth kebabs *(Galouti Kebabs)*

Uttar Pradesh is renowned for its kebabs and here is one example of the many varieties. The term 'Galouti' actually means 'melt in the mouth'. This would be an opportunity for me to impress you with my extensive linguistic skills and explain the etymological derivation of the word Galouti. Unfortunately, I don't have a clue which of the many languages or dialects it comes from. All I know is that it describes these kebabs perfectly.

| | | | |
|---|---|---|---|
| 450 g (1 lb) | **lean minced lamb** | 6 | **mint leaves** |
| 2 | **cloves** | 1/2 bunch | **fresh coriander** |
| 4 | **cardamom pods** | 1 tbsp | **fresh pineapple juice** |
| 1/2 | **blade of mace** | few strands | **saffron** *soaked in milk for 10–15 minutes* |
| 1 tsp | **cumin** | | **salt** |
| 1 cm (1/2 inch) | **cinnamon stick** | | **chilli powder** *to taste* |
| 1 | **star anise** | | |
| 65 g (2 1/2 oz) | **ghee or butter and oil** | | **for the garnish** |
| 1 | **onion** *finely chopped* | | **cucumber** *peeled and cut into ribbons* |
| 1 cm (1/2 inch) piece | **fresh ginger** | | **carrot** *grated* |
| 4 | **garlic cloves** | | **lime juice** *freshly squeezed* |

**serves 4**  Dry roast the cloves, cardamom, mace, cumin, cinnamon and star anise in a pan for a few seconds, then grind them in a coffee grinder or pestle and mortar.

In a separate pan, heat a tablespoon of the ghee and sauté the onion until softened. Put the onion and spices, plus all the other ingredients except for the lamb and the remaining ghee in a food processor, and blitz to a paste.

Spread out the lamb on a flat tray, and pour over the paste of spices. Lightly mix together with a spoon, then leave to marinate, covered, in the refrigerator for 4–6 hours.

Remove the meat mixture from the refrigerator and, with damp hands, shape into patties about 6 cm (2 1/2 inch) in diameter.

Heat the remaining ghee in a heavy-bottomed pan or griddle and cook the patties for a couple of minutes or so on each side, until they are cooked through and have a slightly blackened crust. Serve garnished with the cucumber, carrot and a sprinkling of lime juice.

# potato and lamb cutlets *(Petis)*

A lamb petis is a spicy potato cutlet stuffed with minced lamb. It is good either as a starter or as a snack and goes well with many chutneys; try Tamarind Chutney (page 138) or Coriander and Walnut Chutney (page 137) as an accompaniment. If you're having a drinks party, make them bite-sized and serve as canapés.

| | | | |
|---|---|---|---|
| 4 large 1 kg (2¼ lb) | **potatoes** | | **for the filling** |
| | **ground black pepper** | 225 g (8 oz) | **minced lamb** |
| 1 tsp | **nutmeg** | 2.5 cm (1 inch) piece | **fresh ginger** *finely grated* |
| 1 tsp | **salt** | 2 | **garlic cloves** *crushed* |
| 2–3 | **eggs** | 2 tsp | **ground cumin** |
| Pinch | **ground turmeric** | 1 tsp | **garam masala** |
| | **fresh breadcrumbs** *enough to coat* | 1 small | **onion** *finely chopped* |
| | *the cutlets* | 2 tbsp | **fresh coriander** *finely chopped* |
| | **oil** *for frying* | 2–4 | **green chillies** *(depending on their strength* |
| | **lemon wedges** | | *and how hot you like it), finely chopped* |
| | | 1 tsp | **ground cinnamon** |
| | | 1 tsp | **allspice** |
| | | 2 tbsp | **toasted pine nuts** |

**serves 6–8**  Peel and boil the potatoes until tender, then drain and mash, season with the pepper, nutmeg and salt to taste, and set aside to cool.

Meanwhile, put the lamb in a separate pan with enough water to cover. Cook on a medium-to-high heat, removing any scum that comes to the surface. Add the ginger, garlic, cumin and garam masala, plus salt to taste. Lower the heat and cook for a further 20–25 minutes, stirring occasionally, until all the water has evaporated. Put to one side and leave to cool.

Place the onion, coriander, green chillies, cinnamon, allspice and pine nuts in a large bowl and add the cooled mince mixture, and salt to taste if necessary. Combine thoroughly. Divide the potato mixture into approximately 18 balls, then shape each one into a flat, circular disc. Place a generous teaspoon of the mince in the centre of each disc, then lift the edges up and over the mince and reshape; put to one side.

Break the eggs into a separate bowl, add the ground turmeric and some salt, and beat well. Dip each cutlet in the egg mixture and then coat in the breadcrumbs. Heat some oil in a wide, deep frying pan, then add the cutlets, taking care not to crowd the pan. Fry evenly on both sides, then drain on kitchen paper. Serve either hot or cold, garnished with wedges of fresh lemon.

# chilli and coriander prawn fritters

For a luxurious afternoon snack or starter, try these wonderfully tasty deep-fried king prawns, coated in a piquant batter. They're superb with Tamarind Chutney (page 138).

| | | | |
|---|---|---|---|
| *100 ml (3$^1$/$_2$ fl oz)* | **full fat milk** | *bunch* | **fresh coriander** *chopped* |
| *pinch* | **ground saffron** | *200 g (7 oz)* | **gram flour** *sifted* |
| *12 extra large* | **raw king prawns** *peeled and de-veined* | *2 tbsp* | **cornflour** |
| | **salt** | *2 tsp* | **dried mint** |
| | **freshly ground black pepper** | *2 tsp* | **chilli powder** |
| *2.5 cm (1 inch) piece* | **fresh ginger** *finely grated* | *200 ml (7 fl oz)* | **fizzy water** |
| *1* | **garlic clove** *crushed* | *1* | **lime** *juiced* |
| *1 tsp* | **ground turmeric** | | **vegetable oil for deep frying** |

**serves 4**  Pour the milk into a bowl, add the saffron and leave to infuse. Place the prawns in a bowl and season lightly with salt and black pepper. Add the ginger, garlic, turmeric and a few pinches of the coriander and mix well. Cover and leave to marinate in the refrigerator for 20–30 minutes.

Meanwhile, in a large bowl, mix together the gram flour, the cornflour, dried mint, chilli powder and the rest of the coriander. Make a well in the centre. In a jug mix together the fizzy water and lime juice, then add the saffron milk. Immediately pour the liquid, in a steady stream, into the well, whisking until you have a smooth batter.

Heat the oil for deep frying in a wok. As soon as it is hot, dip the prawns into the batter and then deep fry them in the oil until golden brown all over. Remove with a slotted spoon, drain on kitchen paper and serve hot.

**cook's note**  You must remember two things when cooking the fritters: the oil should be hot but not smoking, so that you hear a crackling sound when you drop the prawns in. Secondly, it is important to be quick when using the batter since much of the crispiness of the fritters comes from the gas in the fizzy water.

# duck samosas

Samosas are a street food, but I wanted to take them upmarket. Given that peacock and humming bird are so hard to find, I settled for duck, and, though I say it myself, it works very well, especially with the Grenadine and Orange Dip (page 140).

| | |
|---|---|
| 1 | **skinless duck breast (Barbary or Gressingham)** *weighing about 170 g (6 oz) trimmed of fat and diced* |
| 1 tbsp | **oil plus extra for deep frying** |
| 1/2 tsp | **cumin seeds** |
| 2 medium | **red onions** *chopped* |
| 1 | **green chilli** *de-seeded and chopped* |
| 1 tsp | **garam masala** |
| 1/4 tsp | **ground turmeric** |
| | **salt** |
| 1 tbsp | **fresh coriander** *chopped* |
| 2 | **spring onions** *chopped* |
| 115 g (4 oz) | **plain flour** |
| 12 sheets | **samosa pastry** *(see notes on ingredients)* |

**makes 10–12**    Heat the oil in a wok or frying pan that can be subsequently covered with a lid. As soon as it is hot, add the cumin seeds and wait for them to crackle. Add the onions, and cook until they become translucent. Now add the duck, and continue to cook on a high heat until the meat begins to brown. Add the chilli, garam masala, turmeric and some salt and mix well, then reduce the heat, cover, and cook for 5 minutes. Add the coriander and spring onions, remove from the heat and set aside to allow the mixture to cool.

Mix the flour with 50 ml (2 fl oz) water to make a paste. Fold one of the pastry sheets in half to make a strip. Place a spoonful of the duck mixture in one corner, then fold the pastry over to make a triangle. Continue to fold the triangle along the strip, sealing the edges with the flour-and-water paste. Repeat the process until all the filling has been used.

Heat the oil for deep frying in a deep-fat fryer or wok until hot. You can test to see if it is hot enough by dropping a small piece of pastry into the oil – if it sizzles immediately and starts to change colour after a few seconds, it's ready. Fry the samosas in batches until golden brown, remove with a slotted spoon and drain on kitchen paper. Serve hot with the dip.

# crab samosas

Samosas are usually made with meat or vegetables, but I thought it was time they got a makeover, so we made them with crab for the restaurant and tried them out on our unsuspecting customers. They were a huge hit and the comedian Sanjeev Bhaskar found them dangerously irresistible when we were filming *Delhi Belly*. Serve with Tomato and Chive Dip (page 142).

| | |
|---|---|
| 200 g (7 oz) | **fresh crabmeat** *flaked (thawed if frozen)* |
| 1 tbsp | **vegetable oil plus extra for deep frying** |
| 1 tsp | **mustard seeds** |
| 6–8 | **curry leaves** |
| 1 tsp | **ground turmeric** |
| 2 cm (1 inch) piece | **fresh ginger** *finely grated* |
| | **salt** |
| 2 tsp | **green or red chillies** *finely chopped* |
| 1 small bunch | **fresh coriander** *finely chopped* |
| 12 sheets | **samosa pastry** |
| 115 g (4 oz) | **plain flour** |

**makes 10–12**  Heat the oil in a heavy-bottomed frying pan. Add the mustard seeds, curry leaves, turmeric and ginger, and fry, stirring frequently, for 1–2 minutes, until fragrant. Add the crabmeat, a pinch of salt, the chillies and the coriander, mixing well, and cook for a further 2–3 minutes.

Mix the flour with 50 ml (2 fl oz) water to make a paste. Take one of the sheets of pastry and fold it in half to make a strip. Place a spoonful of the crab mixture in one corner and fold the pastry over to make a triangle. Continue to fold the triangle along the strip, sealing the edges with the flour paste when you reach the end. Repeat the process, making 10–12 samosas in all.

Heat the oil for deep frying in a deep-fat fryer or wok until hot. You can test to see if it is hot enough by dropping a small piece of bread into the oil – if it sizzles immediately and starts to change colour after a few seconds, it's ready. Fry the samosas in batches until golden brown, remove with a slotted spoon and drain on kitchen paper. Serve hot with the dip.

# chapati

The chapati suffers from an identity crisis. So often it's treated as an afterthought, yet it is as much a part of the Indian diet as bread is in the West. It's great for dipping in dals and raitas, and for mopping up thick, rich sauces. It is also a good alternative if you're not in the mood for rice. As a child, I fulfilled my Enid Blyton fantasies by having chapatis spread with lashings of butter and sprinkled with sugar and cinnamon. But while she wrote about The Famous Five, my four siblings and I were The Infamous Five. Sadly, we didn't have a dog, so we made do with an elephant who was rubbish at fetching sticks.

This is a very easy way of preparing chapatis. The dough can be made in advance and kept refrigerated for 2–3 days. Make sure, though, that it is well wrapped in cling film or inside a plastic food bag.

| | |
|---|---|
| *400 g (14 oz) flour* | **chapati flour** |
| *¹/₂ tsp* | **salt** |
| *230 ml (8 fl oz)* | **boiling water** |
| *1 tbsp* | **vegetable or corn oil** |

**makes 10–12**   Put the flour and salt in a bowl. Using the handle of a wooden spoon (to avoid scalded fingers), make a well in the flour and gradually pour in the boiling water, stirring continuously to incorporate the flour. Don't panic if the mixture becomes lumpy. Gather the mixture together with your hands and knead until pliable, adding the oil bit by bit. Allow to cool for 30 minutes.

Take a handful of dough and roll into a ball the size of a lime. Repeat until the dough has been used (you should end up with 10–12 balls). Roll out each ball into a disc approximately 18 cm (7 inches) in diameter.

Place an unridged, flat griddle or frying pan on a high heat until hot. Lower the heat to medium, place a chapati on the griddle and dry fry until cooked through. When the colour of the bread changes, flip it over to cook the other side. At this point it will bubble and puff out. Now take a spatula and, starting at the edges, gently press the chapati back down on to the pan, to make sure the bottom cooks through. Both sides should have little brown spots. Make all the chapatis in the same way, stacking them as they are done, wrapped in a clean cloth to keep warm. You can reheat the chapatis in the microwave or oven.

Monsoon season on the Fulham Road.

# pooris

For those of you who have been longing for something deep fried, the wait is over. These are a bit of a paradox – or, to get a bit literary, an oxymoron. Although they're deep fried, they're very light and puffy in texture. Serve with Aloo Panchporan (page 111) and natural yoghurt, or with Shrikand (page 163).

| | |
|---|---|
| *225 g (8 oz)* | **chapati flour** |
| *115 g (4 oz)* | **plain flour** |
| *1 tsp* | **salt** |
| *¹/₂ tsp* | **baking powder** |
| *230 ml (8 fl oz)* | **warm water** |
| *1 tsp* | **vegetable oil plus extra for deep frying** |

**makes 20–24**  Sift both types of flour into a large bowl. Add the salt and baking powder. Make a well in the centre with the handle of a wooden spoon, then gradually pour in the warm water, stirring continuously to amalgamate the flour. Using your hands, knead the mixture together, then add the teaspoon of oil and continue to knead until the dough is soft and pliable. Leave to stand for an hour. If you like, the dough can be wrapped in cling film and kept refrigerated for use later.

Take a handful of dough and roll it into a ball the size of a lime. Repeat until all the dough has been used (you should end up with 20–24 balls). On a lightly floured surface, roll out each ball into a pancake roughly 12.5 cm (5 inches) in diameter. It's best to prepare six pancakes at a time, because the actual frying of the pooris is very quick.

Heat the oil in a deep frying pan until hot. If the oil is not hot enough, the poori will not puff up, so check the temperature by dropping a small piece of raw dough into the oil; if it sizzles and rises to the surface, it is ready. Fry each poori separately, turning as soon as it puffs up to cook the other side – this will only take about 10 seconds. Remove with a slotted spoon and serve immediately.

# basic paratha

Parathas are thick layered breads basted with butter or ghee. Once you have tried your hand making this foolproof, basic paratha, you can experiment with various fillings. This is a wonderful bread to have for breakfast, for lunch or as part of a main meal. It's impossible not to get mucky making it, but it is fun to have a go at doing so with the family, especially the kids. Best eaten hot.

| | |
|---:|:---|
| 100 g (3 1/2 oz) | **plain flour** |
| 400 g (14 oz) | **chapati flour** |
| 1/2 tsp | **salt** |
| 350 ml (12 fl oz) | **hot water** |
| 30 ml (1 fl oz) | **oil** |
| | **ghee or vegetable oil** |

**makes 10–12**   Combine both types of flour in a large bowl, add the salt and mix together with your fingers. Make a well in the centre and gradually pour in the water, stirring to amalgamate it with the flour. It's best to use the handle of a wooden spoon to do this, as it will prevent you scalding your fingers, plus it gives you greater control over where the flour is falling. Don't panic if the mixture becomes quite lumpy. Add the oil, which will help bind the dough, then roll up your sleeves, and start mixing and kneading with your hands until the dough is smooth and pliable and comes clean away from the sides of the bowl. Allow to cool for 45–60 minutes. Cover with cling film.

Divide the dough into 10–12 equal portions, and roll each into a ball about the size of the palm of your hand. Lightly dust a work surface with flour, and roll out each ball into a circle roughly 20 cm (8 inches) in diameter. Brush each of the circles with some melted ghee or oil and sprinkle with some flour, roll up into sausage shapes, then coil into pinwheels. Finally, roll out the pinwheels into circles 18 cm (7 inches) in diameter. It is this technique that gives the paratha its layers.

Heat a frying pan or flat griddle over a medium flame and, when hot, add a paratha and cook for about a minute until brown spots appear. Turn over and cook for a minute on the other side. Add a teaspoon of ghee to the pan and cook for a further 2–3 minutes until golden. Turn over and cook again on the other side, adding more ghee if necessary. Make all the parathas in the same way, stacking them as they are done, wrapped in a clean cloth to keep warm. You can reheat the parathas in the microwave or oven.

# methi paratha

Yet another take on the paratha, using fresh fenugreek and gram flour.

| | | | |
|---|---|---|---|
| 1 small | **chilli** *finely sliced* | 1 tsp | **ground cumin** |
| $^1/_2$ small | **red onion** *finely chopped* | $^1/_4$ tsp | **ground turmeric** |
| 85 g (3 oz) | **fresh fenugreek leaves** *chopped* | | **salt** |
| 50 g (2 oz) | **gram flour** | 350 ml (12 fl oz) | **hot water** |
| 50 g (2 oz) | **plain flour** | 2 dsp | **vegetable oil** |
| 400 g (13 oz) | **chapati flour** | | **ghee** |
| 1 tsp | **cumin seeds** | | |

**makes 10–12**  Combine the chilli, onion, fenugreek, gram flour, plain flour, chapati flour, cumin seeds, ground cumin, turmeric and 1 level teaspoon of salt in a large bowl. Make a well in the centre, then gradually pour in the hot water, stirring all the time with the handle of a wooden spoon, so that you don't scald your fingers. Using your hands, knead until the dough comes away clean from the sides of the bowl. Now slowly add the oil, to bind the ingredients and give a smooth texture to the dough. Allow the dough to cool for an hour, then place in the refrigerator, wrapped in cling film or a plastic food bag, for 1–2 hours to allow the flavours to infuse.

Remove the dough from the refrigerator and divide into balls the size of a small doughnut. Lightly dust a work surface with flour, then roll out each ball into a circle roughly 20 cm (8 inches) in diameter.

Heat a frying pan or flat griddle over a medium flame and, when hot, add the paratha and cook for about a minute until brown spots appear. Turn over and cook for a minute on the other side. Add a teaspoon of ghee to the pan and cook for a further 2–3 minutes until golden. Turn over and cook again on the other side, adding more ghee if necessary. Make all the parathas in the same way, stacking them as they are done, wrapped in a clean cloth to keep warm. You can reheat the parathas in the microwave or oven.

# paratha with sweet potato filling

Usually, parathas stuffed with plain potatoes and served with yoghurt are eaten at breakfast or teatime. Why not try this alternative, using sweet potatoes? They can be prepared up to a day in advance and kept in the refrigerator until you are ready to cook them.

| | | | |
|---|---|---|---|
| 210 g (7 1/2 oz) | **chapati flour** | | **for the sweet potato filling** |
| 210 g (7 1/2 oz) | **plain flour** | 400 g (14 oz) | **sweet potato** *peeled and chopped* |
| 1 tsp | **salt** | 1 tsp | **salt** |
| 2 tbsp | **ghee** *melted* | 1 tbsp | **vegetable oil** |
| 230 ml (8 fl oz) | **warm water** | 1 tsp | **black mustard seeds** |
| | **ghee or vegetable oil** *for frying* | 1 tsp | **cumin seeds** |
| | | 1 | **red onion** *finely chopped* |
| | | 1/4 tsp | **ground turmeric** |
| | | 1–2 | **green chillies** *de-seeded and finely chopped* |
| | | 1 tbsp | **fresh coriander** *chopped* |

**makes 8**  Combine both flours in a large bowl and add the salt and ghee. Gradually pour in the warm water to form a soft dough (you may find you don't need it all). Lightly dust a work surface and knead the dough until it is smooth and pliable. Cover it with cling film and allow to rest for an hour.

Meanwhile, prepare the filling. Boil the sweet potato until tender, drain well, then mash in a bowl and add the salt. Heat the oil in a frying pan. When it starts to smoke, add the mustard and cumin seeds and allow them to sizzle and pop for 25 seconds, stirring continuously, then add the onion and fry until softened. Now add the turmeric, chillies and coriander and stir. Then add the mashed sweet potato, mix well cook for 2 minutes. Remove from the heat and cool.

Divide the dough into 16 pieces and shape into balls. On a lightly floured surface, roll out each ball into a circle 14 cm (5 1/2 inches) in diameter. As you go, layer the parathas in a stack, separated by cling film. Spread filling over eight of the parathas, leaving a border of 1 cm (1/2 inch). Brush the edges with water and place a plain paratha on top, pressing the edges together to seal them.

Heat a frying pan or flat griddle over a medium flame and, when hot, add a paratha and cook for about a minute until brown spots appear. Turn over and cook for a minute on the other side. Add a teaspoon of ghee to the pan and cook for a further 2–3 minutes until golden. Turn over, cook on the other side, adding more ghee if necessary. Stack the parathas in a clean cloth to keep warm. You can reheat them in the microwave or oven.

**Baby as the Sugar Plum Fairy.** I had a brainwave. What better way to promote the opening of *L'Eté Indien*, our new Indian restaurant, than to call in the services of an elephant? Baby did us proud, though she was the cause of an argument. Was she an Indian or an African elephant? As she pointed out to us, she considers herself a French elephant and couldn't see what all the fuss was about. As revenge for our bickering, she made a good effort at uprooting the tree in the old village square which didn't go down too well with the locals. As Baby would say, *c'est la vie*.

# stuffed paratha parcels *(Petti Pathiri)*

These innovative parcels are very tasty, and transform a simple Indian bread dough into a particularly moreish snack – an exotic second cousin once removed of the Cornish pasty.

| | |
|---|---|
| 225 g (8 oz) | **boneless lamb from the leg** *cut into* |
| | *3 cm (1 1/4 inch) cubes* |
| 1 tsp | **chilli powder** |
| 1 tsp | **ground coriander** |
| 1/4 tsp | **ground turmeric** |
| 2 | **garlic cloves** *crushed* |
| 2.5 cm (1 inch) piece | **fresh ginger** *finely grated* |
| 3 | **hard-boiled eggs** *sliced in half* |
| | **oil for deep frying** |

**for the masala**

| | |
|---|---|
| 2 tbsp | **ghee** |
| 2 small | **onions** *diced* |
| 4 | **green chillies** *chopped* |
| 3 | **garlic cloves** *crushed* |
| 3 cm (1 1/4 inch) piece | **fresh ginger** *grated* |
| 2 sprigs | **curry leaves** *(approx. 12 leaves)* |
| 1 tbsp | **fresh coriander** *chopped* |
| | **salt** |
| 1/2 | **lime** *juiced* |

**for the chapatis**

| | |
|---|---|
| 225 g (8 oz) | **wheat flour or chapati flour** |
| 100 g (3 1/2 oz) | **plain flour** |
| 1/4 tsp | **bicarbonate of soda** |
| 1 dsp | **vegetable oil** |

**makes 6**   Place the meat in a large saucepan and add the chilli, coriander, turmeric, garlic and ginger. Pour over enough water to cover the meat (approximately 500 ml/18 fl oz), cover with a lid, and simmer for 1–1 1/2 hours until the lamb is tender and almost all the liquid has evaporated. Allow the lamb to cool, then, using your fingers, shred into fine pieces. Set aside while you make the masala.

Heat the ghee in a frying pan, then add the onions, chillies, garlic, ginger, curry leaves, coriander and salt to taste. Stir and fry until the onions turn a nutty brown. Add the shredded lamb, together with the lime juice, and continue to fry 1–2 minutes, then remove from the heat. Set aside to cool while you make the chapatis.

Combine the flours with the bicarbonate of soda in a bowl, then add enough water to bind and knead to a firm, smooth dough. Add the oil, to bind the ingredients and ensure a smooth texture. Divide the dough into 12 and roll into balls about the size of a lime.

Lightly dust a work surface with flour and roll out each ball into a circle roughly 10 cm (4 inches) in diameter. Place approximately 2 heaped tablespoons of the filling in the centre of six of the chapatis. Lightly press half a hard-boiled egg, yolk-side down, into the filling. Cover with the remaining six chapatis, pressing down well to seal the edges together. Using a sharp knife or a pastry wheel, trim the edges to make a neat square.

Heat the oil for deep frying in a deep-fat fryer or wok until hot. You can test to see if it is hot enough by dropping a small piece of bread into the oil – if it sizzles immediately and starts to change colour after a few seconds, it's ready. Deep fry the 'parcels' in batches until they are crisp and golden. Drain on kitchen paper and serve straight away.

When boarding-school term ended for the summer break, I'd stay with my relatives near the Western Ghats. Fish was always eaten during the week, leaving poultry and meat for weekends only. Fish and seafood were prepared fresh and grilled. Some fish were sundried to use in curries or made into hot pickles. As you make your way through this section, you will come across some of my favourite recipes.

# FISH

£16.95 Per

LE

TH EAST ATLA

# prawn curry with coconut milk *(Konju Roast)*

I made this dish on a Chinese fishing boat while filming *Coconut Coast* in Kerala. It is distinguished from other prawn dishes by the use of kokum and dried red chillies.

| | |
|---:|:---|
| 4 | **dried red chillies** |
| 1 tsp | **ground coriander** |
| 4 tbsp | **coconut oil or vegetable oil** |
| 3 | **onions** *finely chopped* |
| 3 cm (1 1/4 inch) piece | **fresh ginger** *grated* |
| 3 fat | **garlic cloves** *chopped* |
| 3 sprigs | **curry leaves** *(approx. 18 leaves)* |
| | **salt** |
| 2 | **green chillies** *chopped* |
| 1 walnut-sized piece | **kokum or tamarind** *soaked in 50 ml (2 fl oz) warm water* |
| 450 g (1 lb) | **raw prawns** *shells removed and cleaned* |
| 100 ml (3 1/2 fl oz) | **coconut milk** |

**serves 4** Soak the red chillies in 6 tablespoons warm water for 15 minutes, then pound to a paste with the ground coriander. A pestle and mortar is best for this.

Heat the coconut oil in a large, lidded saucepan, tip in the onions, ginger, garlic and curry leaves. Cook until the onions have browned, then add the red chilli and coriander paste, plus salt to taste. Continue to cook, stirring continuously, over a low heat for 1–2 minutes, then add 150 ml (1/4 pint) water.

Mash the kokum or tamarind into its soaking water, removing any seeds and discarding them. Add to the pan and simmer the sauce until it thickens. This should take about 5 minutes. Add the prawns, cover, and continue to simmer for a further 5–7 minutes until the prawns are just cooked. Pour in the coconut milk and heat through. Check the seasoning and add salt if necessary, then serve.

On the rice boat at sunset cooking the Konju Roast. The boat in the background is a fishing boat with just about the freshest fish you can get, short of raiding your goldfish bowl.

# green spicy king prawns *(Jinga Hara Masala)*

Coconut is the basis for a lot of Keralan cooking and you'll see the similarities between this and some of the other recipes I have included. However, they each have their own distinct taste. Many of the tempering ingredients are also the same; it is the method of cooking that creates the difference. It is the coriander in this recipe that gives it its character and vibrant colour.

If you are short of time, this is a quick and easy dish to prepare, especially if you have cooked prawns in your refrigerator. All you have to do is make the sauce and add the prawns – the result is this wonderful melt-in-the-mouth sensation, perfect with plain boiled rice. If you want something more elaborate, serve it with Fresh Cucumber and Beansprout Salad (page 128) and Lemon and Ginger Rice (page 148).

| | |
|---|---|
| 450 g (1 lb) | **raw king prawns** *de-veined and washed* |
| 3 tbsp | **fresh coriander** *chopped* |
| 2 | **garlic cloves** *finely grated* |
| 2 medium | **green chillies** *chopped* |
| 1 | **lime** *juiced* |
| | **salt** |
| 1 tbsp | **coconut oil or vegetable oil** |
| 100 ml (3 ¹/₂ fl oz) | **coconut milk** |

**for the tempering**

| | |
|---|---|
| 1 tbsp | **coconut oil or vegetable oil** |
| ¹/₄ tsp | **mustard seeds** |
| 1 | **green chilli** *cut into julienne strips* |
| 1 sprig | **curry leaves** |

**serves 4**    Rinse and drain excess water from the prawns, place in a bowl and put to one side. Put 2 tablespoons of the coriander, plus the garlic, chillies, lime juice and some salt in a liquidiser and blend together. Add to the prawns, then leave to marinate for 20–30 minutes.

Heat the oil in a pan until it starts to smoke, then add the marinated prawns and cook for 5–10 minutes depending on whether the prawns are raw or cooked. Raw prawns should take 3–4 minutes longer than the cooked ones. Add the coconut milk and bring to the boil. Lower the heat and simmer for a few seconds.

Heat the tempering oil in a separate pan on a high heat and, when hot, add the mustard seeds, chilli and curry leaves. Stir for a few seconds until the seeds pop. Add to the prawns, garnish with the remaining coriander and serve immediately.

# spiced mussels in a tamarind broth

When in San Francisco at the Fisherman's Wharf, I was so inspired by the abundance of seafood that I wanted to find a way of cooking it using Indian spices – my own version of East meets West. It occurred to me to cook mussels in a spicy tamarind broth, reminiscent of the South Indian soup known as rasam, which uses black pepper and tamarind. In other words, an Indian version of Moules Marinière. Serve either as a starter or as a main course with bread to mop up the juices.

| | |
|---|---|
| 1 kg (2 1/4 lb) | **live mussels in their shells** |
| 1 tbsp | **vegetable oil** |
| 1 | **onion** *diced* |
| 2 | **garlic cloves** *finely chopped* |
| 2 cm (3/4 inch) piece | **fresh ginger** *finely grated* |
| 1 sprig | **curry leaves** |
| | **salt** |
| 1 x 400 g | **can chopped tomatoes** |
| 1 tsp | **chilli powder** |
| 2 tbsp | **tamarind paste** |
| 700 ml (1 1/4 pints) | **fish stock or water** |

**for the spice mix**

| | |
|---|---|
| 1 tsp | **fennel seeds** |
| 1 tsp | **coriander seeds** |
| 1 tsp | **peppercorns** |

**for the tempering**

| | |
|---|---|
| 1 dsp | **oil** |
| pinch | **asafoetida** |
| 1/4 tsp | **mustard seeds** |
| 1 sprig | **curry leaves** |
| 2 | **green chillies** *slit lengthways* |

**for the garnish**

| | |
|---|---|
| 1 tbsp | **fresh coriander** *finely chopped* |
| 1 tbsp | **fresh chives** *chopped* |

**serves 4**
*as a starter*
*or 2 as a main course*

First make the spice mix by dry-roasting the spices in a frying pan on a low heat. Allow to cool, then blend to a fine powder.

Heat the oil in a saucepan, add the onion and fry until golden brown. Add the garlic and ginger, curry leaves, salt and the roasted spice mix, and continue to stir. Now add the tomatoes, together with the chilli powder and tamarind paste, and cook until softened. Add the fish stock (or water), bring to the boil, then leave the soup to simmer until it has reduced by about half.

Strain the entire contents through a sieve, pressing on the ingredients to release all the flavours. Return the strained liquid to the saucepan and bring back to the boil. Add the mussels, cover, and cook for 3 minutes until the mussels have opened. Discard any that remain closed.

Heat some oil in a frying pan, add the asafoetida and mustard seeds, and allow to sizzle. Add the curry leaves and chillies. Fry for 30 seconds, then add to the mussel pan. Serve in individual bowls, garnished with coriander and chives.

On the shores of the Arabian Sea, we came across these wonderful cantilevered fishing nets. They're absolutely amazing. These were introduced into Kerala by the Chinese from the court of Kubla Khan between AD 1350 and 1450. If I were more technical, I'd be able to tell you how they work. Suffice it to say that the stones act as counterweights and the frames are made of teak. I imagine the nets have been changed since 1450, but don't quote me.

# fish kebabs *(Mahi Kebabs)*

A delicious hot and spicy Indian seafood dish that works well with Cucumber Raita (page 133) or Fresh Cucumber and Beansprout Salad (page 128).

| | |
|---:|:---|
| 300 g (10 $\frac{1}{2}$ oz) | **cod fillet** *skinned, boned and cut into 5 mm ($\frac{1}{4}$ inch) dice* |
| 300 g (10 $\frac{1}{2}$ oz) | **salmon fillet** *skinned, boned and finely chopped* |
| 1 | **lime** *juiced, and grated zest* |
| 1 small | **fennel bulb** *finely chopped* |
| small bunch | **fresh coriander** *finely chopped* |
| 4–8 | **green chillies** *finely chopped* |
| 4 | **spring onions** *finely chopped* |
| 2 tbsp | **fennel seeds** *finely ground* |
| 2 tbsp | **coriander seeds** *finely ground* |
| $\frac{1}{2}$ tsp | **salt** |
| 4 | **cloves garlic** *crushed* |
| 5 cm (2 inch) piece | **fresh ginger** *finely grated* |
| 4 tsp | **black peppercorns** *crushed* |

**serves 4**  In a food processor blend half the cod to a smooth paste. Combine this paste with the rest of the chopped cod, salmon and lime zest in a large mixing bowl. Add the fennel, fresh coriander, green chillies, spring onions, fennel seeds, coriander seeds, salt, garlic, ginger, crushed black peppercorns and lime juice, and mix well. Mould the mixture on to 12 skewers, or alternatively shape into fishcakes.

Either grill the kebabs on a barbecue until golden brown on both sides, or shallow fry in vegetable oil.

# scallops in a creamy dill sauce

This sauce has a wonderful flavour, but frankly doesn't measure up as eye candy. The saffron, though, gives it a very stylish golden glow, with a subtle undertone. Given the price of saffron, I probably don't need to tell you to go easy on it. But saffron is also very strong and can be overpowering, so use it sparingly.

| | | | | |
|---|---|---|---|---|
| 8 | **scallops** *cleaned and washed, beards removed* | | | **for the sauce** |
| | | | 1 tbsp | **ghee** |
| pinch | **red chilli powder** | | 1 tsp | **fennel seeds** |
| pinch | **ground fennel** | | 1 | **clove garlic** *crushed* |
| | **salt and freshly ground black pepper** | | 2.5 cm (1 inch) piece | **fresh ginger** *grated* |
| | **oil** | | 1 | **green chilli** |
| | | | 2 | **shallots** *finely chopped* |
| | | | 1 tsp | **wholegrain mustard** |
| | | | 100 ml (3 1/2 fl oz) | **fish stock** |
| | | | 1 | **lime** *zest* |
| | | | 100 ml (3 1/2 fl oz) | **fresh double cream** |
| | | | 3–5 | **strands saffron** *soaked in a tbspn of warm water* |

**for the garnish**
**chopped fresh dill and/or chives**

**serves 2–4**    Marinate the scallops in the chilli powder, fennel and salt and pepper for 10 minutes.

Meanwhile, prepare the sauce. Heat the ghee in a frying pan. When hot, add the fennel seeds and allow them to sizzle. Add the garlic, ginger, green chilli and shallots, stirring continuously. Allow the shallots to soften for a minute or two, then add the mustard, stirring all the time. Gradually pour in the fish stock, then add the lime zest and allow the sauce to reduce slightly. Now add the cream, and the soaked saffron, and let the sauce bubble until you have a nice rich consistency. Leave on a low heat while you prepare the scallops.

Brush some oil on to a griddle or non-stick frying pan and sear the scallops for 20–30 seconds on each side. Remove from the pan and add them to the sauce. Just before serving, garnish with fresh dill and chives.

# salmon with green mango *(Mahi Aam)*

In Keralan households, fish is traditionally cooked in an earthenware pot called a chutty. However, if your local chutty dealer has shuffled off to Chuttyland, a non-stick pan will do just as well. Here I am using green mango, which acts as a souring agent and is widely available in Indian grocers. Try and get the smaller mangoes, which are sharper in taste. Although I have used salmon, any firm fish would be suitable.

| | |
|---|---|
| 4–6 | **salmon steaks or fillets** *approx. 150gm ( 5¹/₂ oz ) each* |
| 1 small | **green mango** *peeled and cut into chunks* |
| 2 | **green chillies** *thinly sliced* |
| 1 tbsp | **vegetable oil** |

**for the coconut paste**

| | |
|---|---|
| 1 cup | **grated coconut** |
| 1 small | **onion** *finely chopped* |
| 1 sprig | **curry leaves** *(approx. 7 leaves)* |
| 1 tsp | **ground coriander** |
| ¹/₂ tsp | **chilli powder** |
| ¹/₄ tsp | **ground turmeric** |
| | **salt** |

**for the tempering**

| | |
|---|---|
| 1 tbsp | **coconut oil or vegetable oil** |
| ¹/₄ tsp | **mustard seeds** |
| ¹/₄ tsp | **cumin seeds** |
| 1 | **green chilli** *thinly sliced* |
| 1 sprig | **curry leaves** *(approx. 7 leaves)* |
| ¹/₂ | **lime** *juiced* |

**serves 4–6**   Put all the ingredients for the coconut paste, plus 180 ml (6 fl oz) water, into a blender and blitz to form a thick paste.

Take a wide, deep, non-stick frying pan, and put in the salmon pieces. Add the mango, chillies and coconut paste, making sure the salmon is evenly coated. Pour in 240 ml (8 fl oz) water, then drizzle the oil over the whole mixture. Gently bring to the boil, then simmer, uncovered, on a medium-to-low heat for up to 10 minutes, or until the fish is just cooked and the mango has begun to turn translucent. Turn the fish over to finish cooking.

Pour the tempering oil into a separate frying pan and place on a high heat. Add the mustard and cumin seeds and fry until they begin to pop and sizzle. Add the chilli and curry leaves, and stir for a few seconds. Pour over the fish, then drizzle over the lime juice. Serve immediately.

Here on Kathur Beach in Mararikulum the fish — anchovies, sardines and pilchards — are laid out to dry. The anchovies are then ground for paste and the other fish for poultry feed. Bizet's Pearl Fishers sprang to mind. I was getting very excited about a lovely matching set of a pearl necklace and drop earrings (for my sisters of course) but all I could offer them was anchovies.

# banana-leaf-wrapped sea bass

Wrapping the sea bass in a banana leaf ensures the fish remains moist, and imparts to it a subtle flavour. Banana leaves can be found in Thai and certain Asian grocers. However, foil can be used as a substitute. A mango and yoghurt dressing works beautifully with this dish, and, together with plain rice and Masoor Dal (page 108), you have a complete meal.

| | | | |
|---|---|---|---|
| 2 | **sea bass fillets,** *each weighing approx.* 150 g (5½ oz) | | **for the dressing** |
| 1 | **banana leaf** *cut into two* | ½ | **green mango** *peeled and chopped* |
| 1 | **garlic clove** *finely grated* | 2 tbsp | **natural yoghurt** |
| 1 cm (½ inch) piece | **fresh ginger** *finely grated* | | **salt** |
| 1 tsp | **chives** *chopped* | 1 tbsp | **vegetable oil** |
| 1 tsp | **green chilli** *finely chopped* | 1 tsp | **mustard seeds** |
| 2 tsp | **fresh coriander** *chopped* | 1 tsp | **chopped curry leaves** |
| | **salt and freshly ground black pepper** | ½ tsp | **asafoetida** |
| 2 pinches | **chilli powder** | | |
| knob | **butter** | | |
| 4 slices | **lime** | | |

**serves 2**   Preheat the oven to 200°C/400°F/Gas Mark 6.

Place the sea bass fillets on the pieces of banana leaf. Sprinkle over the garlic, ginger, chives, chilli, coriander, salt, black pepper and chilli powder. Top with the butter and slices of lime. Fold each piece of banana leaf up over the fish, to form a parcel, and secure with cocktail sticks. Put in a roasting tin, place in the oven and bake for 6–8 minutes.

Meanwhile, mix together the mango and yoghurt in a bowl and season with salt. Heat the oil in a frying pan, add the mustard seeds, curry leaves and asafoetida, and fry, stirring, for 2 minutes, until the mustard seeds begin to pop and the mixture emits a fragrant aroma. Stir into the yoghurt and mango, mixing well.

Remove the banana-leaf parcels from the oven and let them rest for 2 minutes. Unwrap the fish and serve with the mango and yoghurt dressing.

# halibut in tamarind sauce

Don't be put off by the number of ingredients in this dish, or the fact that it needs to be left for 2–3 hours to marinate. The beauty of it is that the ingredients do all the work for you and, having spent 15–20 minutes on the marinade, you can then have a few hours for yourself. So why don't you nip down to D&G for a spot of shopping, although if you can afford that, you've probably got someone else to cook for you. When you return from your retail therapy you'll be ready for the next stage, looking gorgeous in your new outfit.

| | | | | |
|---|---|---|---|---|
| 4 | **halibut steaks** *washed and dried, approx. 175g (6 oz) each* | | | **for the sauce** |
| | | 150 ml (¹/₄ pint) | **vegetable oil** |
| | | 1 small | **onion** *finely sliced* |
| | **for the marinade** | 1 tsp | **cumin seeds** |
| 6 | **garlic cloves** *grated* | 2.5 cm (1 inch) piece | **fresh ginger** *finely grated* |
| 5 cm (2 inch) piece | **fresh ginger** *finely grated* | 2 | **garlic cloves** *finely grated* |
| 1 | **lemon** *juiced* | 2 | **tomatoes** *chopped* |
| ¹/₂ tsp | **ground turmeric** | 1 small | **green pepper** *cut into julienne strips* |
| 2 tsp | **ground coriander** | 2 tbsp | **tamarind concentrate** |
| 1 tsp | **chilli powder** | | |
| 1 tsp | **garam masala** | | **for the garnish** |
| 2 | **green chillies** *finely sliced* | | **fresh coriander** *chopped* |
| 2 | **spring onion** *finely chopped* | | |
| ¹/₂ bunch | **fresh coriander** *finely chopped* | | |
| 1 tbsp | **tomato purée** | | |
| | **salt** | | |

**serves 4**    Combine all the marinade ingredients in a large bowl and mix well. Coat the halibut steaks with the marinade and leave the bowl in the refrigerator for at least 2–3 hours to allow the flavours to infuse.

Heat the oil in a wide, non-stick frying pan, then add the onion and fry until the slices turn a golden brown. Now add the cumin seeds, ginger and garlic and continue to fry, stirring, for 1–2 minutes. Add the tomatoes and green pepper and cook until they start to soften. Add the halibut steaks, along with their marinade, and cook for 4–5 minutes on each side until just cooked through. Finally, add the tamarind and stir for a further 1–2 minutes until it has amalgamated with the sauce. Garnish with the coriander and serve immediately.

This section calls for an awful lot of feather ruffling. I'm going to ruffle yours by not telling you where every dish comes from. And if your life feels incomplete without such knowledge, content yourself with the fact that I have bowed to pressure in other sections of the book, so you'll be able to get your cultural and historical fix there. Besides, all you really need to know about chicken is that, in India, we always use it skinned, to prevent the sauce becoming too fatty. So if you've nothing better to do on a Sunday afternoon, you can always skin a chicken. We don't do slimy, floppy skin. Also, it's always eaten on the bone. If you don't like it like that, feel free to 'chuck dem bones'.

# POULTRY AND GAME

# tandoori chicken

Let's talk tandoori. Put simply, it's a way of baking meat and fish in a vat-shaped clay pot with hot charcoal in it. Tandoori cooking originated on the North West frontier of India. Here endeth the lecture.

I'm going to be strict now. Don't go anywhere near those jars of lurid, sunset-coloured tandoori paste they sell in supermarkets. Steer clear, and that's an order. If you're using whole joints of chicken, or a whole fish, make incisions in the flesh so that the yoghurt and spices are able to penetrate and tenderise the meat. You may be short of the odd vat-shaped clay pot, but don't worry. You can just as easily cook this on a barbecue, under a grill, or in the oven.

Tandoori is usually served with Naan bread, a simple salad and chutney.

| | |
|---:|:---|
| 6 | **chicken breasts on the bone** |
| 3 | **garlic cloves** *finely grated* |
| 2 cm (³/₄ inch) piece | **fresh ginger** *finely grated* |
| 2 tsp | **garam masala** |
| 2 tbsp | **lemon juice** |
| | **salt** |
| 2 pinches | **saffron strands** *soaked in 2 tbsp warm water for 10 minutes* |
| 4 tbsp | **natural yoghurt** |

**serves 6**   In a large bowl, mix together the garlic, ginger, garam masala, lemon juice, salt and saffron. Using a sharp knife, make three or four slashes across each of the chicken breasts, then place them in the bowl, making sure to rub the marinade into the cuts. Cover and marinate in the refrigerator for 30 minutes, then add the yoghurt, mixing it in thoroughly. Re-cover and return to the refrigerator to marinate overnight.

Preheat the oven to 230°C/450°F/Gas Mark 8. Place the chicken breasts on a rack in a roasting tin, put on the top shelf of the oven and roast for 15–20 minutes, until the chicken is thoroughly cooked, turning the breasts over halfway through the cooking time.

# chicken tikka

Indians simply don't do chicken tikka masala, so no way am I going to go there. Tikka are boneless pieces of meat marinated in yoghurt and spices, and then cooked in a clay oven, but this recipe works just as well in an oven, under a grill, or even on a barbecue. Serve it with any type of salad and breads. The marinade is simplicity itself to prepare — the only thing you need to do is to fry the onions, which takes about 15 minutes, the rest is blended in a food processor. It can also be prepared in advance, if you so wish.

| | |
|---|---|
| 450g (1 lb) | **boneless chicken** cubed |
| 1 small bunch of | **fresh coriander** chopped |
| 1 tbsp | **onions** fried to a golden brown |
| $^1/_2$ tsp | **salt** |
| 2 cm ($^3/_4$ inch) piece | **fresh ginger** finely grated |
| 2 | **garlic cloves** finely grated |
| 4–6 | **green chillies** chopped |
| 100 ml (3 $^1/_2$ fl oz) | **natural yoghurt** |
| 100 ml (3 $^1/_2$ fl oz) | **single cream** |
| $^1/_2$ | **lime** juiced |
| 1 tsp | **garam masala** |

**serves 4**  Put the coriander, fried onions, salt, ginger, garlic, chillies, yoghurt, cream and lime juice in a food processor and blend to a smooth paste. Place the chicken in a large bowl, add the marinade and mix thoroughly. Sprinkle over the garam masala, cover with cling film and marinate in the refrigerator overnight.

Preheat the oven to 200°C/400°F/Gas Mark 6. Spread out the chicken evenly in a roasting tin, and roast in the oven for 10–15 minutes until the chicken is cooked through. Serve hot.

# wood pigeon with mustard *(Junglee Kabutar Sarsonwala)*

Pigeons are eaten throughout the Indian subcontinent. This recipe, which Chef Brinder has devised at the Star of India, includes the use of mustard oil and mustard, hence the term *Sarsonwala* – made of mustard. The longer the pigeons are allowed to marinate, the more tender and flavoursome they become. If you can't get pigeon, you could try this dish using quail.

You need to start this dish a day before to drain the yoghurt and marinate the birds.

| | |
|---|---|
| 4 | **wood pigeons** |
| 1 tbsp | **mustard oil** |
| 1 tbsp | **sunflower oil** |
| 2.5 cm (1 inch) piece | **fresh ginger** *grated* |
| 4 | **garlic cloves** *crushed* |
| 1 tbsp | **grain mustard** |
| | **salt** |
| 1 tsp | **garam masala** |
| 1 tsp | **chilli powder** |
| $^1/_2$ tsp | **ground turmeric** |
| 4 tbsp | **Greek yoghurt** *(drained overnight in a colander lined with either muslin or a J-cloth)* |
| 1 | **lemon** *juiced* |
| | **fresh coriander leaves** *to garnish* |

**serves 4**  Skin the wood pigeons, wash them in cold running water, then dry with kitchen paper. Cut into four pieces (two breasts and two legs). Using a sharp knife, make gashes to enable the spices to penetrate. Whisk together all the remaining ingredients except the coriander in a bowl, then smear this marinade over the pieces of wood pigeon. Cover and leave to marinate in the refrigerator overnight.

Preheat the oven to 200°C/400°F/Gas Mark 6. Place the wood pigeon in a roasting tin and bake for 20 minutes, then leave to rest in a warm place for 5–10 minutes before serving. Serve garnished with the coriander, accompanied by a green salad.

# cardamom chicken curry

Sweet-scented cardamom lends an intriguing flavour to this simple curry. The idea for it came to me while I was in a cardamom plantation during the filming of *Coconut Coast*. There was this chicken, and there was I under the cardamom tree. So I said to the chicken, 'There ain't nobody here but us, chicken. Let's get cooking!'

| | | | |
|---|---|---|---|
| 1 | **chicken** *weighing about 1 kg (2¹/₄ lb), skin removed and jointed into 8 pieces, or 8 skinless chicken joints* | | **for the garnish** |
| | | | **freshly ground black pepper** |
| 75 ml (3 fl oz) | **vegetable oil** | ¹/₄ tsp | **ground cardamom** |
| 6 | **cardamom pods** *split lengthways* | 2 tbsp | **fresh coriander** *chopped* |
| 3 cm (1 ¹/₄ inch) piece | **fresh ginger** *peeled and shredded* | | |
| 2 fat | **garlic cloves** *chopped* | | |
| 2 | **green chillies** *shredded* | | |
| 2 medium | **onions** *diced* | | |
| 1 sprig | **curry leaves** *(approx. 12 leaves)* | | |
| | **salt** | | |
| ¹/₂ tsp | **ground turmeric** | | |
| ¹/₂ tsp | **chilli powder** | | |
| 1 tsp | **ground coriander** | | |
| 1 tsp | **ground cardamom** | | |
| 450 g (1 lb) | **tomatoes** *finely chopped* | | |

**serves 4–6**   Heat the oil in a large pan and toss in the cardamom pods. After a few seconds they will begin to sizzle and give off a lovely nutty aroma. As soon as this happens, stir in the ginger and garlic, followed by the chillies, onions and curry leaves. Add a pinch of salt, to speed up the browning of the onions, and fry them over a medium heat until golden.

Sprinkle in the turmeric, chilli powder, ground coriander and half the ground cardamom. Stir and fry for a further minute, then add the tomatoes and 150 ml (¹/₄ pint) water. Continue to cook until the sauce has thickened slightly. Add the chicken joints into the pan, plus a dash of water, sprinkle in the remaining ground cardamom, and simmer for 20–30 minutes until the chicken is tender and the sauce has thickened further.

Serve garnished with a few grindings of black pepper, a little more ground cardamom and scattered with chopped fresh coriander.

# chicken cooked with coco

There are lots of ways of cooking chicken with coconut milk. This is my ver.
with spices, chillies, fresh coriander and coconut milk. Perfect with plain ric
parathas. Khoa can be found in most Asian grocery shops. Alternatively, you
it entirely, which would make for a lighter dish.

| | |
|---|---|
| 4 | **skinless chicken breasts** |
| 3–4 | **garlic cloves** *finely grated* |
| 2 cm ($^3/_4$ inch) piece | **fresh ginger** *finely grated* |
| few pinches | **ground cardamom** |
| | **freshly ground black pepper** |
| 2–3 tbsp | **ghee** |
| | **salt** |
| 2–3 tbsp | **natural yoghurt** |
| $^1/_2$ block | **khoa** *grated* |
| 165 ml | **coconut milk** |
| 5–6 | **whole green chillies** *pricked with a fork* |
| small bunch | **fresh coriander** *finely chopped* |

**serves 4** Place the chicken in a large bowl. Add the garlic, ginger, cardamom and a pinch of pepper. Mix well, cover and marinate in the refrigerator for 30 minutes to 1 hour.

Melt the ghee in a deep, heavy-bottomed frying pan and brown the chicken pieces on all sides. Add the salt, yoghurt and khoa. Cook briskly for about 20 minutes, stirring often, until the sauce has reduced and dried, then lower the heat. Add the coconut milk and chillies and stir well. Simmer for a few minutes more. Garnish with coriander and serve.

# dak bungalow chicken

...itha gave me this recipe while filming *Coconut Coast*. She was about to get married, having met ...fiancé on the internet. She casually dropped into the conversation that 4,000 of her closest friends would be invited. I was so overwhelmed that I forgot to ask her where this dish originated. Dak bungalows are travellers' rest houses, made famous by Kipling and still to be found here in this green and pleasant land.

Curry leaves, coconut and hints of star anise are put to very good use here. Use a non-stick pan as the coconut absorbs the oil and could burn the pan.

| | |
|---|---|
| 1 small | **chicken** *skin removed and jointed into 8 pieces* |

**for the spice paste**

| | |
|---|---|
| 1 tbsp | **coconut oil** |
| 3 cm (1 1/4 inch) | **cinnamon stick** |
| 1/4 tsp | **peppercorns** |
| 1 | **star anise** |
| 2 | **dried whole red chillies** |
| 2 | **shallots** *sliced* |
| 85 g (3 oz) | **grated coconut** |
| 1/2 tsp | **salt** |
| 6 | **curry leaves** |
| 1 tbsp | **coriander seeds** |

**for the masala sauce**

| | |
|---|---|
| 3 tbsp | **coconut oil** |
| 1 | **onion** *sliced* |
| 4 cm (1 1/2 inch) piece | **fresh ginger** *shredded* |
| 3 fat | **garlic cloves** *roughly chopped* |
| 1 sprig | **curry leaves** *(approx. 12 leaves)* |
| | **salt** |
| 1/2 tsp | **turmeric** |
| 1/2 tsp | **chilli powder** |

**for the garnish**

| | |
|---|---|
| 2 tbsp | **vegetable oil** |
| 1 | **onion** *sliced* |
| 1 sprig | **curry leaves** |
| 3 | **whole red chillies** *tops removed* |
| handful of | **coriander** *chopped* |

**serves 4**  First, make the spice paste. Add the coconut oil to a frying pan and place over a medium heat. Toss in the cinnamon, peppercorns, star anise and chillies. After a few seconds, add the shallots, coconut, salt, curry leaves and coriander seeds. Stir and fry until the coconut turns a lovely nut-brown colour. Remove from the heat, allow to cool slightly, then grind to a fine paste in a pestle and mortar or in a coffee grinder. Set aside while you make the masala sauce.

Heat the oil in a large pan, then add the onion, ginger, garlic and curry leaves, plus a pinch of salt. Stir and fry over a low heat for about 15 minutes, until the onion has browned. Sprinkle in the turmeric and chilli powder and stir to mix while still on the heat. Add the spice paste and stir-fry for about 5 minutes to allow the flavours to infuse.

Add the chicken pieces to the pan, together with 175 ml (6 fl oz) water. Simmer until the chicken is tender and the sauce has thickened. If the sauce becomes too dry before the chicken is cooked, add a dash or two of water.

Heat the oil for the garnish in a separate frying pan, toss in the onion and fry until pale gold, then add the curry leaves and chillies. Spoon the chicken on to a platter and garnish with a tangle of fried onion, curry leaves, red chillies and chopped coriander.

Baby took a shine to Sally Ann whom she obviously thought the only other sensible one in the whole adventure. This was our version of a dramatic reconstruction of Hannibal's entry into France. Our motley crew, who were involved in setting up the restaurant, pose in front of L'Eté Indien.

# chicken dhansak

This is a typical Parsee dish, *dhan* meaning rice and *sak* meaning vegetables. (As you may already know, the Parsees fled to India from Persia to avoid religious persecution and settled mainly in Gujarat and Maharashtra.) It was a very popular dish at the Star of India during the 1950s and '60s, when it was served with pillau rice, though I recommend the more authentic Chilgoza Rice (page 146) as the perfect accompaniment.

There's a long list of ingredients, but if you get everything measured, prepared and lined up before you even get your pans out of the cupboard, you will find that the method is straightforward. If any of you were boy scouts or girl guides, your old motto 'Be Prepared' will stand you in good stead here!

Use a total of 300 g (10$^1$/$_2$ oz) toor dal if the other dals are not readily available. You should be able to find most dals, however, as well as ready-made dhansak masala, tamarind paste and jaggery, at Asian grocers.

| | | | |
|---|---|---|---|
| 1.25 kg (2 lb 12 oz) | **chicken** *cut into 6–8 pieces* | 100 ml (3 $^1$/$_2$ fl oz) | **oil** |
| 600 ml (1 pint) | **chicken stock** *made with the bones, neck, giblet and trimmings, or water* | 2 tsp | **dried fenugreek leaves** (kasturi methi) |
| 1 tbsp | **moong dal** | 1 tsp | **ground cumin** |
| 1 tbsp | **masoor dal** | 3 tsp | **ground coriander** |
| 1 tbsp | **urad dal** | 2 tsp | **red chilli powder** |
| 200 g (7 oz) | **toor dal** | 3 | **tomatoes** *chopped* |
| 50 g (2 oz) | **tamarind paste** | 2 | **green chillies** *chopped* |
| 2 large | **onions** *chopped* | 1 tbsp | **jaggery** |
| 200 g (7oz) | **red pumpkin or butternut squash** *roughly diced into 1 cm ($^1$/$_2$ inch) cubes* | 1 | **lime** *juiced* |
| 150 g (5 $^1$/$_2$ oz) | **aubergine** *roughly diced into 1 cm ($^1$/$_2$ inch) cubes* | | **for the dhansak masala** |
| 5 cm (2 inch) piece | **fresh ginger** *finely grated* | 1 $^1$/$_2$ tsp | **garam masala** |
| 6 | **garlic cloves** *crushed* | $^1$/$_2$ tsp | **star anise** |
| good cupful of | **coriander leaves** *chopped* | $^1$/$_4$ tsp | **ground nutmeg** |
| $^1$/$_2$ tsp | **turmeric** | $^3$/$_4$ tsp | **ground fenugreek** |
| 2–3 sprigs | **fresh mint** *(approx. 20 leaves)* | $^1$/$_2$ tsp | **ground black mustard** |
| | **salt** | $^1$/$_2$ tsp | **ground pepper** |
| | | 1 tsp | **red chilli powder** |

**serves 6–8**  Wash the dals together in lukewarm water, then rinse and soak in cold water for 30 minutes. Soak the tamarind in 200 ml (7 fl oz) of water for at least 30 minutes.

Pour 700 ml (1¼ pints) water into a large, lidded pan, and add the drained dal, along with the onions, pumpkin and aubergine. Add a third of the ginger, half the garlic, plus 1 tbsp of the coriander and turmeric and a sprig of mint. Bring to the boil, cover, and simmer until the dal has softened. Season with one teaspoon of salt. Allow to cool slightly, then beat with a hand whisk to achieve a creamy consistency.

While the dal is cooking, heat the oil in a large frying pan and fry the remaining ginger and garlic, the remaining chopped fresh coriander and the remaining mint. Then add the dried fenugreek leaves, all the spices for the dhansak masala, ground cumin, ground coriander, red chilli powder, tomatoes and green chillies, and fry for 2 minutes, stirring continuously.

Add the chicken, sauté for 2 minutes, season with salt and stir well. Add the chicken to the dal along with the chicken stock or water. Add the jaggery and leave to simmer for about 30–45 minutes until the chicken is cooked through. Before serving, add the tamarind water and lime juice, adjust the salt to taste, simmer for a couple of minutes and serve.

# duck varuval

Chef Brinder decided to give this famous South Indian dish from Tamil Nadu a bit of a makeover. Traditionally it is made with chicken. *Varuval* in Tamil means 'curry', and it is distinguished by its use of fennel seeds, curry leaves, mustard seeds and black pepper. It has become a signature dish at the Star of India. I have adapted it here for home cooking. The sauce would work beautifully with a firm white fish.

| | |
|---|---|
| 4 | **Gressingham or Barbary duck breasts with skin** *weighing approx. 175 g (6 oz) each* |
| | |
| | **for the marinade** |
| ¹/₂ | **lemon** *juiced* |
| 1 x 2.5 cm (1 inch) piece | **fresh ginger** |
| 4 | **garlic cloves** |
| 1 tsp | **chilli powder** |
| 1 tbsp | **vegetable oil** |
| | **salt** |

| | |
|---|---|
| | **for the sauce** |
| 2–3 tbsp | **vegetable oil** |
| pinch | **asafoetida** |
| 1 tsp | **mustard seeds** |
| 2 sprigs | **curry leaves** *(approx. 15 leaves)* |
| 1 tsp | **fennel seeds** |
| 4 medium | **onions** *finely diced* |
| 4 | **tomatoes** |
| 2 tbsp | **tomato purée** |
| 1 tsp | **chilli powder** |
| 1 tsp | **garam masala** |
| 2 tbsp | **single cream** |

**serves 6–8**

Trim the duck breasts of silverskin. Using a sharp knife, score the top fat in a criss-cross pattern, taking care not to cut into the flesh. Mix all the marinade ingredients to make a paste. Rub this into the duck breasts and leave covered in a bowl to marinate in the refrigerator overnight.

Preheat the oven to 200°C/400°F/Gas Mark 6. Take an ovenproof frying pan large enough for the duck breasts. Heat the oil in the pan and add the breasts skin-side down. Sear them until the skin is well browned. Turn the breasts over and transfer the pan to the oven. Roast for 10 minutes so that the flesh is still pink in the middle. Cover with foil to keep warm and leave to rest for 5 minutes.

Meanwhile, heat the oil for the sauce in a sauté pan. Add the asafoetida, mustard seeds, curry leaves and fennel seeds, let them sizzle, and continue to stir. Now add the onions and cook until golden brown. Add the tomatoes, tomato purée, chilli powder and garam masala. Reduce the heat and cook for 5 minutes until the sauce has a rich consistency.

Pour off the duck fat from the pan and add any residual juices to the sauce and mix well. Stir in the cream. Serve the duck sliced on a bed of the sauce.

If there are any vegetarians reading this, now is the time for you to go and walk the dog, because this chapter is all about meat. It's for committed carnivores only. So think of this as the X-rated part of the book.

Most of the recipes are lamb-based, but I have also added beef and a venison dish. As in Britain, venison is not standard fare in India, but it is available. However, if you happen to spot a passing deer just consider how delicious it could be on your plate. Forget all images of Bambi.

The Beef Coconut Stew comes from Kerala, where we filmed *Coconut Coast*. I think of it as an Indian version of goulash, without the Hungarian elements, that uses coconut instead of paprika.

Most of the lamb dishes are ones I was brought up with, the others are classic recipes from the Star of India. Traditionally, lamb is cooked on the bone, because doing so gives the flavour an extra kick, and makes the dishes very rich and meaty, but if you prefer to use boneless lamb, that's fine too.

# MEAT

# beef coconut fry

Kerala is a beautiful state in South India, famous for its lagoons and waterways. It has a very specific cuisine, of which this dish, flecked with curry leaves, coconut and softened shallots, is a perfect example.

| | |
|---|---|
| 750 g (1 lb 10 oz) | **beef stewing steak** cubed |
| 2 | **onions** sliced |
| 3 cm (1 1/4 inch) piece | **fresh ginger** shredded |
| 3 fat | **garlic cloves** |
| 2 sprigs | **curry leaves** (approx. 14 leaves) |
| 3 | **green chillies** shredded |
| 50 ml (2 fl oz) | **coconut oil or vegetable oil** |

**for the spice mix**

| | |
|---|---|
| 3 | **dried red chillies** |
| 2 tsp | **coriander seeds** |
| 1 tsp | **ground turmeric** |
| 3 cm (1 1/4 inch) | **cinnamon stick** |
| 1/2 tsp | **black peppercorns** |
| 3 | **cloves** |

**to finish**

| | |
|---|---|
| 3 tbsp | **coconut oil or vegetable oil** |
| 4 | **shallots** sliced |
| 1 | **red pepper** sliced |
| 1–2 sprigs | **curry leaves** (approx. 12 leaves) |
| | **freshly chopped coriander** |
| 2 tbsp | **toasted coconut** |

**serves 4–6**

First, make the spice mix. Put the chillies, coriander seeds, turmeric, cinnamon, peppercorns and cloves in an electric grinder and process until you have a fine powder. Alternatively, use a pestle and mortar.

Put the beef in a large, heavy-bottomed, lidded saucepan, add the onions, ginger, garlic, curry leaves, chillies and coconut oil and mix well. Add the spice mix, and pour in just enough water to barely cover the meat. Cover and simmer on a low heat for about 2 hours until the beef is tender. If it becomes too dry, add a little more water to prevent the meat from sticking.

To finish, heat the coconut oil in a frying pan and add the shallots, red pepper and curry leaves. Allow them to soften for 5–10 minutes, then add the coriander and the toasted coconut. Add to the cooked beef and fry until almost all the liquid has evaporated.

# spiced whole leg of lamb *(Sabut Raan)*

This dish can be made either in the oven or cooked on the hob, whichever is more convenient. It could be described as an exotic alternative to the British roast, the main difference being the infusion of spices and the succulent texture achieved by allowing the flavours to marinate for several hours. In India, a whole leg of lamb is an indulgence, so it is usually only cooked in affluent households, or on special occasions.

| | | | |
|---|---|---|---|
| 1.75–2.25 kg (4–5 lb) | **whole leg of lamb** *excess fat trimmed* | 1 tsp | **whole peppercorns** |
| 3 | **garlic cloves** *finely grated* | 1 tsp | **whole coriander seeds** |
| 8 cm (3 inch) piece | **fresh ginger** *finely grated* | 8 cm (3 inch) | **cinnamon stick** |
| 2 tbsp | **green papaya** *finely grated ( optional)* | 2 | **bay leaves** |
| 4 tbsp | **natural yoghurt** | | |
| 1–2 tsp | **salt** | | **for the garnish** |
| 50 ml (2 fl oz) | **oil** | 2 | **fresh tomatoes** *quartered* |
| 2 medium | **onions** *weighing about 225 g (8 oz), sliced* | | **fresh coriander** *finely chopped* |
| | | 2 | **green chillies** *sliced into julienne strips* |
| | **for the spice mix** | 3 | **spring onions** *coarsely chopped* |
| 1 tsp | **cloves** | | |

**serves 6–8**  First make the spice mix by dry roasting the cloves, peppercorns, coriander seeds, cinnamon and bay leaves in a non-stick pan until lightly browned. Allow to cool, then grind to a fine powder, either in an electric grinder or in a pestle and mortar.

Put the garlic, ginger and papaya in a large, shallow bowl, add the yoghurt and salt to taste, mix well, then add the spice mix. Using a sharp knife, make incisions all over the lamb. Place in the bowl and rub the marinade into the meat, making sure it penetrates the gashes, then marinate for 2–4 hours or overnight in the refrigerator. The longer the meat marinates, the better the flavour.

Preheat the oven to 200°C/400°F/Gas Mark 6. Put the lamb in a greased roasting tin. Heat the oil in a frying pan, and fry the onions until golden brown, then pour both the oil and the onions over the lamb, reserve some for garnishing. Pour 450 ml ($^3/_4$ pint) water into the roasting tin, cover with foil, and place in the oven. Roast for a total of 2–2$^1/_2$ hours, until the joint is completely tender and cooked evenly throughout. Reduce the oven temperature to 180°C/350°F/Gas Mark 4 after 20 minutes, and turn the joint over every 20 minutes, basting it to keep the meat moist. Forty-five minutes before the end of the cooking time, remove the foil in order to brown the joint. Add garnish ingredients to the roasting tin 5 minutes before the end of cooking time. Allow the meat to stand, covered loosely with foil, for 15 minutes before carving. Serve with the garnish and reserved onions.

Beauty and the Beast? I met Lakshmi the elephant when the crew and I were staying in Serenity, a glorious hotel in Kerala. All I can say is that it was love at first sight. Lakshmi is definitely the girl for me. She used to be a circus elephant but now spends her time sunbathing with a long, cool cocktail by her side.

# lamb in black pepper sauce *(Gosht Kali Mirch)*

After a hectic schedule filming in Kerala, I came back with something special for my sister Farah, in the form of the Tellicherry pepper, one of the finest, high-grade peppercorns. Months later, I was visiting my sister's house, when she served up this very tasty lamb dish. I asked her what she had put in it. I shouldn't have been surprised when she revealed that she had used the peppercorns I had brought back for her from my trip. What made the dish so fantastic was the combination of aromatic black spices and the use of whole and ground Tellicherry peppercorns.

 I couldn't believe how quickly it was wolfed down by my nieces and nephews. Unless you've just returned from a holiday in Kerala, however, you'll have to make do with ordinary black peppercorns. Fortunately, they work perfectly well.

| | | | |
|---|---|---|---|
| 450 g (1 lb) | **leg of lamb** *cubed* | 2 medium | **tomatoes** *finely chopped* |
| 75 ml (3 fl oz) | **vegetable oil** | 4 | **green chillies** *finely chopped* |
| 2 medium | **red onions** *finely chopped* | 2 tsp | **freshly ground black pepper** |
| 1 large | **black cardamom** | $^1/_4$ tsp | **garam masala** |
| 3 | **cloves** | 1 tbsp | **natural yoghurt** |
| 4 | **green cardamom pods** | | |
| 2 x 5 cm (2 inch) | **cinnamon sticks** | | **for the garnish** |
| 1 dsp | **black peppercorns** | $^1/_2$ | **lemon** *juiced* |
| | **salt** | 2 tbsp | **fresh coriander** *chopped* |
| 2 | **garlic cloves** *finely chopped* | | |
| 4 cm (1$^1/_2$ inch) piece | **piece fresh ginger** *finely grated* | | |

**serves 4**   Heat the oil in a large, lidded, pan, add the onions and the black cardamom, cloves, green cardamom, cinnamon, peppercorns and a pinch of salt. Fry until the onions turn a deep golden brown. Stir in the garlic and ginger, plus the tomatoes, chillies, black pepper and garam masala. Continue to stir for a minute or two, to allow the spices to infuse. Now mix in the yoghurt.

 Add the lamb, coat it with the spice mixture, and cook on a medium-to-high heat for 5 minutes. Add 300 ml ($^1/_2$ pint) hot water, cover, and bring back to the boil. Reduce the heat and cook for a further 1–1$^1/_2$ hours until the lamb is tender and has absorbed all the flavours. Stir occasionally to prevent the meat from sticking. Once the meat is tender, raise the heat and reduce the volume of liquid until the oil separates from the sauce. Just before serving, squeeze over the lemon juice and garnish with the chopped coriander.

# lamb with pickling spices *(Achari Handi)*

A succulent and robust spiced dish that is wonderful to eat on an Indian summer's day. Achari means pickling and the five spices in the recipe are common pickling spices. A suitable accompaniment would be Chapatis (page 37) and one of the many relishes that are included in this book.

| | | | |
|---|---|---|---|
| 450 g (1 lb) | **leg of lamb** *cubed, but keep the bone* | 3 x 2.5 cm (1 inch) | **cinnamon sticks** |
| 75 ml (3 fl oz) | **vegetable oil** | 4 | **whole cloves** |
| 30 ml (1 fl oz) | **mustard oil** | 4 | **whole green cardamoms** |
| | | 5 | **onions** *sliced* |
| | **pickling spices** | 4 | **garlic cloves** *crushed* |
| 1 tsp | **mustard seeds** | 4 cm (1 1/2 inch) piece | **fresh ginger** *finely grated* |
| 1/2 tsp | **fennel seeds** | 1 tsp | **chilli powder** |
| 1/2 tsp | **nigella seeds (kalongi)** | 1 tsp | **garam masala** |
| 1/2 tsp | **cumin seeds** | 1 tsp | **ground cumin** |
| 1/2 tsp | **fenugreek seeds** | 1 tsp | **ground coriander** |
| | | 1 tsp | **ground turmeric** |
| | | | **salt** *to taste* |
| | | 1 1/2 tbsp | **tomato purée** |
| | | 1 | **lemon** *juiced* |

**serves 4** Heat the two oils in a saucepan until hot. Add the mustard seeds and, as soon as they start to splutter, add the fennel, nigella, cumin and fenugreek seeds, and continue to sauté until they start to crackle. Add the cinnamon, cloves, cardamoms and onions, and fry until golden brown. Add the garlic and ginger and fry for 2–3 minutes. Now add the remaining ground spices, plus salt to taste. Continue to stir for a further 3–4 minutes, then add a cup of water to prevent the spices from sticking. Finally, add the meat, along with a further 300 ml (1/2 pint) water. Bring to the boil, reduce the heat to a simmer, cover and cook for about an hour until the meat is tender. Stir in the tomato purée and lemon juice and adjust the seasoning. Reduce the sauce if it seems too thin. Serve hot with chapatis or Chilgoza Rice (page 146).

# lamb cooked in a white sauce (Saphed Gosht)

In Hindi, *saphed* means white, so guess what colour the ingredients in this dish are? Very good – white. This is a very rich dish. No, I can't lie to you: it's fattening. Rich is a polite way of saying loaded with calories. But get over it; it's worth it , plus you might as well get carried away and have it with Chapatis (page 37) and Aloo Panchporan (page 111).

| | | | |
|---|---|---|---|
| 450 g (1 lb) | **boned leg of lamb** cut into 5 cm (2 inch) cubes | 2 tsp | **desiccated coconut** |
| 2 tbsp | **ghee** | 120 ml (4 fl oz) | **milk** |
| 2 tbsp | **yoghurt** | 15 g ( 1/2 oz) | **khoa (milk powder)** |
| 2 | **red chillies** seeds, flesh reserved for garnish | 1 tsp | **rosewater** |
| 5 cm (2 inch) piece | **fresh ginger** peeled and grated | 1/2 | **lime** juiced |
| | **salt** | 1 tsp | **ground cardamom** |
| 1 tbsp | **almonds** blanched | 1 tbsp | **fresh coriander** chopped |
| 2 tsp | **white poppy seeds** | | |

**serves 4–6** Put the meat in a saucepan, cover with cold water, add a pinch of salt and bring to the boil. Remove any scum that rises to the surface and simmer for 5–7 minutes. Keep removing as much scum as possible. Drain the meat and rinse in fresh water.

In a separate pan, heat the ghee along with the yoghurt, chilli seeds, ginger and some salt. Add the lamb and stir for a few minutes over a medium heat to coat the meat with the spices. Add enough water to just cover the meat – about 300 ml ( 1/2 pint) – bring to the boil, then simmer for 45–60 minutes, until tender.

Put the almonds, poppy seeds, coconut and half the milk in a liquidiser and blend to a smooth paste. Stir the paste into the meat, along with the remaining milk and the milk powder, and heat through, then lower the heat to a gentle simmer to prevent curdling (see cook's note). When the sauce has thickened to a gravy consistency, and the fat has separated from the sauce, add the rosewater, lime juice and ground cardamom.

Garnish with the chilli and chopped coriander and serve immediately.

**cook's note** If the sauce curdles, remove the meat with a slotted spoon and allow the sauce to cool. Pour the curdled sauce into a food processor or liquidiser and blend to a smooth consistency. Return the sauce to the pan, add the meat, and heat very gently until the oil separates.

This is me in a Brad Pitt moment, though he's rarely seen with beetroot. A lovely dish on the shore of Coconut Lagoon. I'm talking about the beetroot thoran, of course, but thanks for thinking of me. In case you think we've crossed the border into Poland, beetroot is a widely used ingredient in Indian cooking. The French Bean and Cashew Nut Thoran recipe on page 122 can also be made with beetroot.

# lamb with fenugreek *(Methi Gosht)*

Methi Gosht has always been one of the most popular dishes at the Star of India. It is a very earthy lamb dish, enhanced with the flavours of fresh and dried fenugreek. I simply love it with plain rice and Masoor Dal on page 108.

| | | | |
|---|---|---|---|
| 1 kg (2 1/4 lb) | **leg of lamb** *cut into 5 cm (2 inch) cubes* | 2 | **garlic cloves** *finely grated* |
| 85 g (3 oz) | **methi (fresh fenugreek)** *thick stalks removed* | 1/2 tsp | **chilli powder** |
| | **vegetable oil** | 1 tsp | **ground cumin** |
| 2–3 | **whole cardamoms** | 1 tsp | **ground coriander** |
| 4 | **cloves** | 1 tsp | **salt** |
| 2 | **bay leaves** | 1 dsp | **tomato purée** |
| 2 medium | **onions** *sliced* | 1 tbsp | **kasturi methi (dried fenugreek)** |
| 1/2 tsp | **ground turmeric** | | **fresh coriander** *chopped, to garnish* |
| 5 cm (2 inch) piece | **fresh ginger** *finely grated* | | |

**serves 4–6**  Bring 200 ml (7 fl oz) water to the boil in a small saucepan, add the fresh methi leaves and cook for about 5 minutes. Strain, reserving the water for later use. Chop the blanched methi leaves and keep to one side.

Heat 3–4 tablespoons of oil in a saucepan, add cardamoms, cloves and bay leaves and when they crackle add the onions and turmeric and fry until golden brown and caramelised. Now add the cubed lamb, and brown on all sides. Add the ginger and garlic and continue to fry for 5 minutes. Now add the chilli powder, ground cumin, ground coriander, salt, and a dash of water, and stir, making sure you incorporate the spices from the bottom of the pan. Now add the tomato purée and the reserved methi water made up to 400 ml (14 fl oz) with fresh water. Bring to the boil and simmer until tender, about 1 hour.

In a frying pan, dry fry the kasturi methi until toasted. Add it to the meat along with the reserved blanched methi, and continue to cook on a low heat for 5 minutes, to allow the flavours of the two forms of methi to infuse.

Serve garnished with some chopped coriander.

# lamb pasanda

Let's bring clarity to 'the Pasanda'. I don't know what you thought a pasanda was, but let's get this straight: it is a flattened meat, like an escalope. Clear? It can be marinated in any type of marinade – sweet, spicy, rich, creamy, whatever. But let me reiterate, it is 'Flat Meat'. This version is one of my favourites. Perfect with Chilgoza Rice (page 146).

| | | | |
|---|---|---|---|
| 450 g (1 lb) | **lean lamb fillet** *cut into 2 inch (5 cm) squares, 1 cm (¹/₂ inch) thick* | ¹/₂ tsp | **saffron strands** *soaked in warm water* |
| 100 g (3¹/₂ oz) | **ghee** | 230 ml (8 fl oz) | **natural yoghurt** |
| 4 x 5 cm (2 inch) | **cinnamon sticks** | 2–3 | **onions** *sliced, then fried until golden brown* |
| 4 | **whole black cardamoms** | 1 tbsp | **grated fresh ginger** |
| | **fresh coriander** *chopped* | 6 | **garlic cloves** *crushed* |
| | | 2 tsp | **salt** |
| | **for the marinade** | 2–3 tsp | **red chilli powder** |
| 6–8 | **dried figs** *soaked in water for 30 minutes* | 4 tsp | **ground coriander seeds** |
| | | 2 tsp | **garam masala** |
| 1 tbsp | **raisins** *soaked in water for 30 minutes* | 2 tsp | **ground cumin** |
| 2–3 tbsp | **khoa** | 1 tsp | **ground cardamom** |

**serves 4–6** Place the lamb between sheets of cling film and beat flat with a meat hammer or rolling pin.

Grind the marinade ingredients to a fine paste in a food processor. Rub into the lamb, making sure the meat is well coated, and leave for at least an hour.

Melt the ghee in a heavy-bottomed pan, wide enough to take the meat in one layer, and add the cinnamon sticks and black cardamoms. Allow them to sizzle for a few seconds, then add the meat, along with its marinade, spreading it evenly over the base of the pan. Cover with a tightly fitting lid, sealing the edges with a flour and water paste in order to retain all the flavours in the pan. (Alternatively, cover the pan with kitchen foil before putting on the lid, to create a seal.) Cook on a very low heat for 1 hour. If, after this time, the sauce is too thin, raise the heat and reduce the sauce until it has thickened slightly and the oil has separated. Serve garnished with chopped coriander.

My escape route from the more difficult customers.

Meat flattening in the early Iron Age.

# venison pasanda *(Hiran ke Pasanda)*

Brinder, my chef at the Star of India, introduced this dish a while ago and it's already a big favourite. First flatten your deer . . . I don't care how you flatten it dears, under your yoga mat, mattress or following the illustration opposite!

| | | | | |
|---|---|---|---|---|
| 450 g (1 lb) | **venison striploin** | | ¹/₂ tsp | **chilli powder** |
| 60 ml (2¹/₂ fl oz) | **vegetable oil** | | 1 tsp | **ground turmeric** |
| 1 tsp | **fennel seeds** | | 1 tsp | **ground cumin** |
| ¹/₂ tsp | **fenugreek seeds** | | 1 tsp | **ground coriander** |
| 3 | **bay leaves** | | 1 tsp | **garam masala** |
| 3 x 4 cm (1¹/₂ inch) | **cinnamon sticks** | | ¹/₂ tbsp | **tomato purée** |
| 2 | **star anise** | | 1 tbsp | **chopped fresh coriander** |
| 4 | **green cardamom** | | | |
| 6 medium | **onions** *thinly sliced* | | | **for the garnish** |
| 5 cm (2 inch) piece | **fresh ginger** *finely grated* | | 1 large | **potato** *peeled, cut into julienne strips* |
| 2 | **garlic cloves** *finely grated* | | | **oil** |
| | **salt** | | | |

**serves 6**  Remove the skin and membrane on the venison, then cut in slices roughly 1 cm thick. Place the venison between sheets of cling film and beat flat with a meat hammer or rolling pin. Heat the oil in a heavy-bottomed pan, add the fennel and fenugreek seeds, bay leaves, cinnamon, star anise and cardamom, allow to crackle, then add the onions and fry until a pale golden brown. Add the ginger and garlic and cook for a minute or two. Add the venison slices, and brown on both sides, then add the ground spices, plus salt to taste, and cook for 2–3 minutes. Once the spices have coated the venison, pour in 230 ml (8 fl oz) water, lower the heat and simmer for 7–8 minutes. Add the tomato purée and cook for a further minute. Sprinkle the chopped coriander on top and remove from the heat.

Meanwhile, heat the oil in a separate frying pan, then fry the potato juliennes until pale gold and crisp. Drain on kitchen paper and lightly salt. Serve the venison topped with the straw potatoes.

# meatballs in a green sauce *(Koftas Hara Masala)*

This dish is a popular favourite at dinner parties, largely because it produces a fabulous result with minimum effort. Served with Lemon and Ginger Rice (page 148), it is a marriage made in heaven (well, in your kitchen actually).

**for the koftas**

| | |
|---|---|
| 450 g (1 lb) | **minced lamb** |
| 2–3 | **spring onions** *finely chopped* |
| 2 | **green chillies** *finely chopped* |
| 1 tbsp | **fresh coriander** *chopped* |
| 1 tsp | **ground allspice** |
| 1 tsp | **ground cinnamon** |
| 1 tsp | **garam masala** |
| 1 tsp | **freshly ground black pepper** |
| 2 | **garlic cloves** *finely grated* |
| 5 cm (2 inch) piece | **ginger** *finely grated* |
| | **salt** |

**for the sauce**

| | |
|---|---|
| 100 ml (4 fl oz) | **vegetable oil** |
| 3 medium | **onions** *finely sliced* |
| 150 ml (¼ pint) | **natural yoghurt** |
| 3 | **green chillies** |
| small bunch | **fresh coriander** |
| 1 tbsp | **fresh mint** *chopped* |
| 2 | **garlic cloves** *finely grated* |
| 5 cm (2 inch) piece | **fresh ginger** *finely grated* |
| 1 tsp | **ground cumin** |
| 1 tsp | **garam masala** |
| 1 tsp | **ground fennel** |
| | **salt** |
| | **freshly ground black pepper** |
| ¼ tsp | **ground turmeric** |
| ½ | **lemon** *juiced* |

**for the garnish**

| | |
|---|---|
| 1 tbsp | **fried onions** *(see method)* |
| handful | **toasted flaked almonds** |
| 2 tbsp | **single or double cream** |
| 1 tbsp | **fresh mint** *chopped* |

**serves 4–6** Combine the ingredients for the koftas in a large bowl, mixing thoroughly. Shape into meatballs about the size of a golf ball. Keep to one side.

Heat the oil in a non-stick pan, add the onions and fry until golden brown. Remove with a slotted spoon, reserving the oil in the pan, and drain on kitchen paper. Set aside a tablespoon for the garnish. Put the rest of the onions in a blender or food processor, along with the remaining sauce ingredients, and blend to a smooth paste.

Reheat the oil used to fry the onions, add the paste and cook for 2–5 minutes, then pour in 700 ml (1¼ pints) hot water and bring to the boil. When the sauce is bubbling, add the meatballs. Return to the boil, lower the heat, partially cover with a lid, and simmer for 30–45 minutes until the sauce has thickened and the oil has begun to separate. To serve, drizzle over the cream and garnish with the reserved fried onions, toasted flaked almonds and some fresh mint.

# Haleem

This is a typical Muslim dish, especially popular during the month of Ramadan. If you're not meant to eat for a month between sunrise and sundown, you want something that will keep you going. Haleem is a mouth-watering dish that's not only full of nutrients, but also comforting and exceedingly rich. Just what you need after a heavy day of fasting.

What is so lovely about it is the array of garnish ingredients spread out on your dining table. The whole family gets involved preparing their own portions, adding whatever garnish they prefer: chopped coriander, chopped chillies, fried onions, lemon juice, julienne of ginger, chopped mint.

It's hard to describe the texture of Haleem; what you're aiming for is something between porridge and soup, thick and creamy.

| | |
|---|---|
| 1kg (2 1/4 lb) | **boned leg of lamb** cut into 1 cm (1/2 inch) cubes, plus the bone |
| 6 tbsp | **ghee oil and butter** |
| 5 large | **onions** finely chopped |
| 5 | **cardamom pods** |
| 4 x 5 cm (2 inch) | **cinnamon sticks** |
| 1 tsp | **whole black peppercorns** |
| 5 | **cloves** |
| 2 | **garlic cloves** finely grated |
| 2.5 cm (1 inch) piece | **fresh ginger** finely grated |
| 115 g (4 oz) | **white urad lentils** |
| 115 g (4 oz) | **chana dal** |
| 225 g (8 oz) | **bulgur wheat** |
| 1–2 tsp | **chilli powder** |
| 1 tsp | **ground turmeric** |
| 2 tsp | **ground cumin** |
| 1 tsp | **garam masala** |
| 1 1/2 tsp | **salt** |

**for the garnish**

| | |
|---|---|
| 3 | **onions** thinly sliced then fried until brown and crisp |
| 8–10 | **green chillies** finely chopped |
| 1/2 bunch | **fresh coriander** finely chopped |
| 1/2 bunch | **fresh mint** finely chopped |
| 10 cm (4 inch) piece | **fresh ginger** cut into julienne strips |
| 2 | **lemons** juiced |

**serves 6–8**  Rinse both types of lentil in cold water, then soak in warm water for 30 minutes.

Meanwhile, heat the ghee in a large, heavy-bottomed, non-stick saucepan with a lid. Add the onions and all the whole spices, and sauté until the onions are golden brown. Now add the garlic and ginger and soften for a few minutes. Add the lamb and stir to combine the ingredients. Cook on a medium heat for 30 minutes or so, stirring constantly to prevent sticking, until all the meat is evenly browned and the liquid has evaporated.

Add the soaked lentils to the meat and mix well. Add 500 ml (18 fl oz) water, cover the pan and continue to cook on a medium heat for 20–30 minutes.

Add the bulgur wheat, chilli powder, turmeric, cumin, garam masala and salt, and mix thoroughly. When the bulgur wheat starts to swell and has absorbed most of the moisture in the pan, stir in a further 1 litre ($1^3/_4$ pints) hot water. As soon as the water starts to boil, reduce the heat as low as possible (use a heat diffuser if you have one), cover, and simmer very gently for $2$–$2^1/_2$ hours, stirring occasionally to prevent sticking. Add more hot water (up to 1 litre/$1^3/_4$ pints) whenever the mixture seems too dry. After this time, the meat should be tender enough for you to be able to crush it against the side of the pan with a teaspoon.

Remove the pan from the heat, then, using a hand whisk, beat vigorously until the meat has been broken down and mixture is the texture of porridge. If you prefer, you could leave some chunks of meat; it is up to you how smooth you want it. Spoon into a serving dish, garnish with the fried onions, chillies, coriander, mint and ginger, and sprinkle over the lemon juice. Alternatively, serve the accompaniments in separate bowls, as I prefer to do, so that everyone can help themselves.

India is a vegetarian's paradise. And even if you're a meat-eater, you'll find it hard to resist the huge variety of vegetable dishes on offer.

All the dishes here can be served either as a main meal, or as side dishes. The added bonus is that they're so easy to prepare. OK, I lied. A couple of them may take two episodes of your favourite programme to prepare but, I promise you, they're worth it. You'll also feel virtuous that you're getting your quota of veggies for the day. So, pack your passport and welcome to Vegistan . . .

# VEGETABLES

# spicy red lentils *(Masoor Dal)*

I have two takes on dal: dull dal and darling dal. Dull dal because a watery, green, bland version was served three times a day at boarding school, which made things a tad tedious. So, needless to say, I was put off it for a while. However, darling dal is one of the most versatile, delicious, nourishing, comforting and affordable dishes in the Indian repertoire, and it is the one by which I judge all restaurants.

| | | | |
|---|---|---|---|
| 175 g (6 oz) | **masoor dal** | | **for the tempering** |
| ¼ tsp | **turmeric** | 2 tbsp | **ghee** |
| 1 medium | **onion** *grated* | 1 small | **onion** *sliced* |
| 3 | **garlic cloves** *sliced* | 3 | **garlic cloves** *slivered* |
| 1 tsp | **salt** | 1 tsp | **cumin seeds** |
| 1 small | **green mango** *peeled and sliced; do not discard the stone* | 1 tbsp | **fresh coriander** *chopped* |
| | | 1 | **green chilli** *slit lengthways* |

**serves 4–6**    Wash the lentils, then put in a pan with 400 ml (14 fl oz) cold water. Bring to the boil, remove any scum that comes to the surface, lower the heat and simmer, covered, for about 40 minutes until the lentils have softened and fluffed up. Halfway through the cooking time, add the turmeric, onion, garlic, salt and the mango, plus its stone. Remove the pan from the heat, take out the mango stone and, using a hand whisk, beat the lentils until they are smooth.

Melt the ghee for the tempering in a hot frying pan, add the onion and fry until golden. Stir in the garlic, followed by the cumin and then the coriander and chilli. Stir for a few seconds, add to the cooked dal, and serve.

# creamy black lentils *(Maa Ki Dal)*

*Maa Ki Dal* means 'mother of dals'. The recipe comes from the Punjab and it is a very rich and earthy dish. Traditionally, it is cooked on burning embers but, if you're short of those, it works just as well on the hob. Depending on your viewpoint, it is either a cream dream or a nightmare. If you're going to worry about calories, you'd be better off with the previous recipe, Spicy Red Lentils.

If you wish, the lentils can be cooked in advance and kept overnight in the refrigerator in a sealed container. Avoid finishing the dish until just prior to serving, however, as it's best not to reheat it once the cream has been added.

| | |
|---|---|
| 100 g (3 1/2 oz) | **black urad dal** |
| 1 tbsp | **vegetable oil** |
| 2 | **garlic cloves** *crushed* |
| 2 cm (3/4 inch) piece | **fresh ginger** *finely grated* |
| 1/2 tsp | **chilli powder** |
| 1/2 tsp | **garam masala** |
| 2 tbsp | **tomato purée** |
| | **salt** |
| 1/2 tsp | **dried fenugreek leaves** *(kasturi methi)* |
| 20g (3/4 oz) | **butter** |
| 50 ml (2 fl oz) | **single cream** |

**for the garnish**
**fresh coriander** *chopped*
**green chillies** *chopped*

**serves 4**  Wash and soak the dal in warm water for 1 hour, then drain and put it in a lidded pan with at least six times the volume of water. Bring to the boil, then lower the heat and simmer, untouched, for at least 2 hours, until the lentils have swollen to double their original size and begin to pop. Avoid allowing the water to evaporate by keeping a tight lid on the pan. The cooking time will vary depending on the quality and age of the dal. It is ready when the lentils are soft.

Heat the oil in a separate, large pan, then add the garlic, ginger, chilli powder, garam masala and tomato purée, plus salt to taste. Stir for a couple of minutes, then add 50 ml (2 fl oz) warm water, continuing to stir in order to incorporate all the spices from the base of the pan. Add the dal, along with all the cooking liquid, and cook for 10 minutes, then stir in the fenugreek and butter. Once the butter has melted, add the cream and simmer until you have a creamy consistency. Adjust the seasoning, garnish with the coriander and chillies, and serve.

# spinach and cheese *(Saag Paneer)*

If you frequent Indian restaurants, you'll be familiar with this classic, all-rounder accompaniment, which works as a neutraliser to the palate, especially with spicy food. Most of the time, though, I'm disappointed by the saag paneers I'm served. Too often they consist of rather rubbery fried cubes of cheese, or resemble spinach soup with pallid croutons. The best way to make it is to grate the paneer into the chopped spinach, adding cream for a velvety finish.

| | |
|---:|:---|
| 450 g (1 lb) | **spinach** *blanched and chopped* |
| 1 tbsp | **vegetable oil** |
| 2 tsp | **whole cumin seeds** |
| 1 medium | **onion** *finely chopped* |
| 2 | **garlic cloves** *finely slivered* |
| pinch | **turmeric** |
| 100 g (3 $^1$/$_2$ oz) | **block paneer** *coarsely grated* |
| 100 ml (3 $^1$/$_2$ fl oz) | **vegetable stock** |
| | **salt** |
| 50 ml (1 $^3$/$_4$ fl oz) | **fresh cream** |
| 1 tbsp | **fresh coriander** *finely chopped* |

**serves 4** Wash the spinach in plenty of cold water, letting any sand sink to the bottom, then rinse and drain well in a colander. Put in a large pan, cover with a lid, and place on a medium heat for 2–3 minutes. The spinach will cook in the steam made by the water clinging to its leaves. As soon as it begins to wilt, stir the top leaves to the bottom. As soon as all the leaves are wilted, remove the pan from the heat and drain, squeezing out as much liquid as possible. Allow the spinach to cool, press out the remaining liquid to get the spinach as dry as possible, and roughly chop.

Heat the oil in a saucepan until hot, then add the cumin seeds and allow them to sizzle. Now add the onion and cook until it becomes translucent in colour. Add the garlic and continue to cook until the onions have softened, then add the turmeric. Stir the spinach into the mixture, continue to cook for a further couple of minutes, then add the paneer and vegetable stock. Adjust the seasoning, pour the cream on to the saag paneer, garnish with the coriander, and serve immediately.

# potatoes tempered with five spices
## (Aloo Panchporan)

A very simple stir-fry using five spices, which adds a little je ne sais quoi to the old pommes frites. You will need only 2 teaspoons of the five-spice mix for the tempering, so keep the rest in an airtight bottle or container and use as and when required. Alternatively, you can buy five-spice mix in any Asian grocers, where it is known as panchporan.

| | |
|---|---|
| 1 kg (2¼ lb) | **potatoes** *peeled and diced into 1 cm (½ inch) cubes* |
| 3 tbsp | **vegetable oil** *or enough to cover the base of your pan* |
| ½ tsp | **turmeric** |
| ½ tsp | **red chilli powder** |
| | **salt** |
| ½ | **lime** *juiced* |

**for the five-spice mix (panchporan)**

| | |
|---|---|
| 1 tbsp | **cumin seeds** |
| 1 tbsp | **fennel seeds** |
| 1 tbsp | **fenugreek seeds** |
| 1 tbsp | **nigella seeds** |
| 1 tbsp | **black mustard seeds** |

**for the tempering**

| | |
|---|---|
| 1 tsp | **vegetable oil** |
| 1 | **green chilli** *finely chopped* |
| 1 tbsp | **fresh coriander** *chopped* |

**serves 4–6**  Pour the oil into a non-stick frying pan, large enough to take all the potatoes without overcrowding, and place on a medium-to-high heat. Add the potatoes and sauté until nearly cooked, then add the turmeric, chilli powder, plus salt to taste, and stir-fry thoroughly until both the potatoes and the spices have cooked through.

Heat the oil for the tempering in a separate, small, shallow frying pan until it begins to smoke, then add 2 teaspoons of the five-spice mix. Allow the seeds to crackle and pop, then add the chilli and coriander. Stir for a few seconds, then pour on to the potatoes. Serve immediately, sprinkled with the lime juice.

**cook's note**  If you wanted to prepare an alternative Sunday lunch with the Spiced Whole Leg of Lamb (page 90) you could toss the potatoes with the oil, turmeric, chilli and salt. Roast in the oven along with the lamb for 20–30 minutes before adding the tempered spices.

# cauliflower with sesame seeds *(Til Ki Gobi)*

Few, if any, poems have been written about the humble cauliflower. Wordsworth, for instance, was more taken with daffodils and you can't really substitute 'a host of boring cauliflowers'. However, by adding a few seeds and spices it becomes a thing of wondrous beauty.

This is a lovely, simple dish and I think it goes really well with Western food, as a vegetable accompaniment to fish, chicken or meat, however it's prepared.

| | |
|---|---|
| 1 medium | **cauliflower** *cut into florets, or 4 baby cauliflower heads weighing approx. 45 gm each* |
| 2 tbsp | **vegetable oil** |
| 1 tsp | **cumin seeds** |
| 2 medium | **onions** *finely sliced* |
| pinch | **turmeric** |
| | **salt** |
| 4 | **dried red chillies** *halved* |
| 1–2 dsp | **sesame seeds** |
| 1 | **garlic clove** *grated* |
| 4 cm (1 ¹/₂ inch) piece | **fresh ginger** *finely grated* |
| 2 | **green chillies** *finely chopped* |
| 1 tbsp | **fresh coriander** *chopped, to garnish* |

**serves 4**   Heat the oil in a wide, non-stick pan until it begins to smoke, then add the cumin seeds and allow them to crackle. Now add the onions, along with a pinch of both turmeric and salt, and stir continuously until the onions turn a pale golden brown. Add the dried red chillies, sesame seeds, garlic and half the ginger, continue to cook for a few moments, then add the cauliflower. Stir gently to coat the cauliflower evenly with the mixture. Cover the pan with a lid and cook the cauliflower on a low heat for 7–10 minutes until just tender. When the cauliflower is almost cooked, remove the lid, increase the heat, add the green chillies and the remaining ginger, and stir briskly. Adjust the salt to taste, garnish with the chopped coriander and serve.

# Afghani aubergine casserole

This is a wonderful way of preparing aubergines. I simply love the luscious texture of it, and the way the combination of sweet, piquant, savoury tomato sauce cooled down with mint yoghurt just melts in the mouth. In the Channel 4 TV series *A Place in France*, I served it to Jeremy and Nikki, a honeymoon couple at the B&B. But don't panic. You are allowed to eat this if you're single.

| | |
|---|---|
| 450 g (1 lb) | **aubergines** *cut into 1 cm (¹/₂ inch) slices, very lightly salted on both sides* |
| 3–4 tbsp | **vegetable oil** |
| 400 g (14 oz) | **can chopped tomatoes, passata, or creamed tomatoes** |
| 2 | **garlic cloves** *crushed* |
| 1 tsp | **sambal oelek or 2 fresh green chillies** *finely chopped* |
| 1 tsp | **ground cumin** |
| 1 tsp | **sugar** |
| small bunch | **fresh mint** *chopped* |
| 200 g (7 oz) | **Greek yoghurt** |

**serves 4–6**

Preheat the oven to 190°/375°F/Gas Mark 5.

Heat 2–3 tablespoons of vegetable oil in a frying pan, then sear the aubergine slices on both sides, in batches, until they turn brown and soft, then remove and drain on kitchen paper. You may find you need to add more oil.

If you are using chopped canned tomatoes, blend them until smooth in a liquidiser or food processor, then sieve to get rid of the seeds. Alternatively, use a bottle of passata or a carton of creamed tomatoes, neither of which will need to be sieved.

In a separate saucepan, heat another tablespoon of oil, add the garlic and tomatoes, and then the sambal oelek, cumin and sugar. Simmer for 15–20 minutes until you have a sauce of a fairly rich consistency.

Spread a third of the tomato sauce evenly over the base of a shallow, ovenproof dish, cover with a layer of aubergine slices and sprinkle with half the mint. Spoon another third of the tomato sauce on top, then repeat the aubergine layer and finish with the remaining tomato sauce. Bake in the oven for about 20 minutes, until heated through.

Meanwhile, whisk together the yoghurt and the remaining mint, and season with salt, pepper and a pinch of sugar. Dollop this on top of the hot aubergine casserole.

# Me in uncharacteristic pose, i.e. in the background.

Jeremy and Nikki were among the first of the paying guests at the B&B and we wanted everything to be just right. Besides designing and virtually building the place, I also had to make the Chicken and Prune Biryani (page 152) and the Afghani Aubergine Casserole (see opposite) for them — chiefly to distract them from the fact that the B&B wasn't nearly ready for guests! As far as I know, they're still married, despite the fact that Nigel Farrell was incapable of leaving them alone throughout their stay.

On a snake hunt at the Chelsea Gardens.

# spiced snake beans

This is a classic recipe from the Tamil Nadu region. South Indian food tends to be lighter than food from the North. It's also spicier, and can easily be incorporated into Thai-style meals as it uses fresh coriander and coconut milk.

French beans are a good substitute if you can't find snake beans, which are often sold in Asian and Thai greengrocers. No snakes were hurt in the making of this dish.

| | |
|---|---|
| 2 tbsp | **ghee or vegetable oil** |
| 1/4 tsp | **asafoetida** |
| 1 tsp | **mustard seeds** |
| 1 tbsp | **fresh ginger** *finely grated* |
| 2 | **garlic cloves** *crushed* |
| 2 | **fresh red chillies** *finely chopped* |
| 1/2 tsp | **fenugreek seeds** |
| 1 sprig | **curry leaves** |
| 450 g (1 lb) | **snake beans** *cut into lengths of approximately 10 cm (4 inches)* |
| 125 ml (4 fl oz) | **coconut milk** |
| | **salt** |
| 2 tbsp | **fresh coriander** *chopped* |

**serves 4–6** Heat the ghee or oil in a wok or large pan. As soon as it starts to smoke, add the asafoetida and the mustard seeds and allow them to pop. Now add the ginger, garlic, chillies, fenugreek seeds and curry leaves and stir for 2 minutes. Add the snake beans and cook for a further 5 minutes, stirring continuously, to coat the beans with the spices. Pour in the coconut milk and simmer until the beans are tender and most of the liquid has evaporated. Season to taste with salt. Just before serving, garnish with the chopped coriander leaves.

# crispy okra *(Bhindi Rajasthani)*

Bhindi, otherwise known as okra or ladies' fingers, tend to be slimy and not to everyone's taste. However, these deep-fried, crisp and deliciously light 'wisps' will convert even the most hard-hearted anti-okran. Wonderful as a side dish with most Indian meals, they also make a spectacular 'nibble'.

|  |  |
|---|---|
| *1 medium* | **red onion** *sliced* |
| *300 g (10 1/2 oz)* | **okra** *finely sliced into julienne strips* |
| *2 tsp* | **chat masala powder** |
| *2 tbsp* | **gram flour** |
|  | **oil for deep frying** |
| *1 tbsp* | **fresh coriander** *chopped* |

**serves 4–6**　Combine the onion and okra with the chat masala powder and gram flour in a large bowl. Heat the oil in a wok. When hot, drop the okra mixture into the oil, a few pieces at a time, avoiding large clumps, and deep-fry until the okra turn crispy and golden. (This should only take a few minutes.) Drain on kitchen paper to remove excess oil, garnish with the coriander and serve.

# cashews in a rich coconut sauce

This delicious, melt-in-the-mouth recipe was introduced to me by my mother. Very popular with the younger generation – it's a particular favourite of my nephews and nieces – it is well worth trying. What is unusual about it is that although the cooking time is 2–3 hours, it requires no attention and simply needs to be left alone. In fact, the more you stir the cashews, the longer the dish takes to cook. If you are short of time, however, it is possible to cook it in a pressure cooker, in which case it will take about 45 minutes.

| | |
|---|---|
| 200 g (7 oz) | **unsalted, unroasted cashew nuts** *soaked overnight in cold water* |
| 50 ml (2 fl oz) | **vegetable oil** |
| 1 large | **onion** *$^3/_4$ blended in a food processor, the remainder finely diced* |
| 2 | **garlic cloves** *crushed* |
| 2.5 cm (1 inch) piece | **fresh ginger** *grated* |
| $^1/_4$ tsp | **turmeric** |
| 1 tsp | **ground coriander** |
| 1 tsp | **ground fennel** |
| 200 ml (7 fl oz) | **coconut milk** (**$^1/_2$ can**) |
| 1 tsp | **sugar** |
| | **salt** |
| 2 | **green chillies** *slit lengthways* |

**serves 6–8**   Rinse the cashews in cold water and drain. Heat the oil in a medium non-stick saucepan, add the diced onion and fry on a low heat for 10–15 minutes until it turns translucent and soft; do not allow it to brown. Now add the garlic and ginger, the blended onion, turmeric, coriander and fennel. Pour in 500 ml (18 fl oz) water and stir well to incorporate all the ingredients. Add the cashews to the pan, return to the boil, lower the heat, cover, then cook slowly for 2–3 hours until the cashews are tender to the touch (try not to stir them at all during this time). When the cashews are soft, add the coconut milk, sugar, salt and chillies, then cook for a further 30 minutes on a low heat. Serve hot.

Heavens! Cupid's very blue from eating too much Cashew Stew.

# french bean and cashew nut thoran
## (Kaju Poshu Thoran)

A thoran is a Keralan stir-fry using freshly grated coconut, the basic spices being mustard seeds, curry leaves and chillies. Further south, towards Tamil Nadu, it is known as a poriyal. You can use numerous other vegetables, for example spinach, beetroot or carrot, as an alternative to the beans.

This was one of the dishes served at the opening party of L'Eté Indien, which featured in *A Place in France*. We were all a bit apprehensive about how our food would be received by the locals in the Ardèche, but, much to our relief, they loved it.

| | |
|---|---|
| 450 g (1lb) | **french beans** |
| | **vegetable oil** |
| 125 g (4½ oz) | **cashew nuts** |
| 2 tsp | **mustard seeds** |
| 1 tsp | **cumin seeds** |
| 2 sprigs | **curry leaves** (approx. 15 leaves) |
| 2 cm (1 inch) piece | **fresh ginger** finely grated |
| 2 | **green chillies** finely chopped |
| 100 g (3½ oz) | **fresh coconut** grated or shaved |
| 1 tsp | **sugar** |
| 1 | **lime** or ½ lemon, juiced |
| ½ bunch | **fresh coriander** finely chopped |

**serves 8**   Top and tail the beans, string and cut into 2.5 cm (1 inch) lengths if necessary, depending on the size and age of the beans. Blanch in boiling salted water for 1 minute. Drain the beans and immediately plunge them into cold water to prevent further cooking and retain their colour. When cold, drain well and pat dry with kitchen paper.

Heat a dessertspoon of oil in a non-stick pan and sauté the cashew nuts until golden. Drain on kitchen paper and set aside.

Pour 2 tablespoons of oil into a non-stick frying pan or wok and place on a high heat. As soon as it starts to smoke, add the mustard seeds, cumin seeds and curry leaves. As soon as they begin to pop and crackle, add the ginger and chillies and stir-fry for a moment or so. Now add the beans and heat through, continuing to stir. Finally, add the coconut, sugar, lime or lemon juice, cashew nuts and chopped coriander. Toss everything together and season with salt to taste. Serve immediately.

# lentil dumplings in a yoghurt sauce
## (Masala Vadai)

A very versatile dish, typical of Indian street food, that can be eaten as a starter, side dish, light lunch or snack. During school holidays in Bombay, we would hang out at the local cafés and food stalls along Chowpatty Beach. One of our favourite snacks was *Masala Vadai*, served in dried-banana-leaf bowls. They would be lovely with both the Tamarind Chutney (page 138) and the Green Chutney (page 136).

**for the dumplings**

| | |
|---|---|
| *75 g (3 oz)* | **toor dal (oiled yellow split peas)** *cleaned and washed* |
| *75 g (3 oz)* | **urad dal (white split lentils)** *cleaned and washed* |
| *75 g (3 oz)* | **chana dal (yellow split peas)** *cleaned and washed* |
| *6–8* | **curry leaves** |
| *1 small to medium* | **onion** *finely chopped* |
| *4* | **green chillies** *finely chopped* |
| *5 cm (2 inch) piece* | **fresh ginger** *finely grated* |
| *¹/₂ tsp* | **asafoetida** |
| *1 small bunch* | **coriander leaves** *finely chopped* |
| | **salt** |
| | **oil for deep frying** |

**for the yoghurt sauce**

| | |
|---|---|
| *700 ml (1 ¹/₄ pints)* | **natural yoghurt** |
| *3 tbsp* | **fresh coconut** *grated* |
| *2–4* | **green chillies** |
| *1 tsp* | **cumin seeds** |
| | **salt** |
| *1–2 tbsp* | **fresh coriander** *chopped, to garnish* |

**for the tempering**

| | |
|---|---|
| *1 tbsp* | **vegetable oil** |
| *1 tsp* | **mustard seeds** |
| *¹/₂ tsp* | **asafoetida** |
| *1 tsp* | **cumin seeds** |
| *4–6* | **curry leaves** |
| *1 tsp* | **urad dal** |
| *1* | **red chilli** *quartered* |

**serves 4–6** First make the dumplings. Soak all three lentils in 1 litre (1³/₄ pints) warm water for 2–3 hours to soften. (This will make it easier to blend them later.) Drain the excess water from the lentils, then place them either in a food processor or a liquidiser and blend to a thick paste-like batter. Add the curry leaves, and continue to blend for a few more seconds. Scrape the batter into a large mixing bowl, and add the onion, chillies, ginger, asafoetida and coriander. Season with salt and combine thoroughly.

Heat the oil in a wok or deep pan until hot. (You can check the temperature of the oil by adding a tiny bit of the batter to it – if the oil is hot enough it should sizzle.) Take a small ladleful of the batter and pour it into the cupped palm of one hand; moisten the other hand with water and shape the batter into a dumpling about the size of a small doughnut. Gently slide the dumpling into the oil and fry until crisp and golden brown, then drain on kitchen paper and set aside. Continue to make dumplings in this way until all the batter has been used (you should have enough to make 15–20).

Next make the sauce. Whisk two-thirds of the yoghurt to a smooth consistency in a mixing bowl. Put the remainder of the yoghurt in a food processor or blender, along with the coconut, chillies and cumin seeds, plus salt to taste. Blend to a very smooth paste. Add this mixture to the yoghurt in the bowl and combine thoroughly. Check the seasoning; if more salt is required, add it now. Leave to one side.

Heat the oil for the tempering until it begins to smoke, then add the mustard seeds and, as soon as they begin to pop and crackle, add the asafoetida, cumin seeds, curry leaves and the urad dal. Continue to fry, stirring continuously, until a lovely nutty aroma exudes from the pan. Now add the red chilli and stir for a few more seconds, then immediately pour this mixture into the yoghurt.

To assemble the dish, spoon half the yoghurt on to an oval dish or serving bowl, arrange the dumplings on top, then spoon over the remaining yoghurt. Garnish with the chopped coriander.

**cook's note** If you can't find the toor dal or chana dal, make up the weight with the urad dal.

There are so many Indian relishes, chutneys and salads that they could make a book in themselves. The ones I've included here are some of my personal favourites. They're **a very good way to whet the appetite** and dip into lots of distinct flavours with chapatis. Traditionally, they're eaten at the same time with the main course.

# SALADS, RELISHES AND SIDE DISHES

# fresh cucumber and beansprout salad

A cool, fresh and healthy salad that goes with anything and everything, and is a particularly good antidote to a hot curry.

| | |
|---|---|
| handful | **fresh beansprouts** washed and soaked for 30 minutes |
| 2–3 tbsp | **fresh coriander leaves** finely chopped |
| 1 large | **cucumber** peeled, seeds removed and finely diced/sliced |
| 2 tbsp | **freshly grated coconut or 3 tbsp desiccated coconut** soaked in warm water for 10 minutes then drained and squeezed dry |
| 1 | **green chilli** finely chopped |
| 1 tbsp | **fresh lemon juice** |
| | **salt** |

**for the tempering**

| | |
|---|---|
| 1 tbsp | **vegetable oil** |
| 1 tsp | **mustard seeds** |
| 1/4 tsp | **asafoetida** |
| 1 tsp | **cumin seeds** |
| 1–2 | **dried red chilli** slit lengthways |
| 1 sprig | **curry leaves** |
| 1 tsp | **white urad dal** washed and dried |
| 1 tsp | **chana dal (yellow split peas)** washed and dried |

**serves 4–6**  In a bowl, combine the coriander, cucumber, coconut, green chilli, lemon juice and salt, to taste. Add the drained bean sprouts and mix thoroughly.

Heat the oil in a heavy frying pan until hot, then add the mustard seeds and allow them to sizzle and pop. Add the asafoetida, cumin seeds, dried red chilli, curry leaves, urad and chana dals. Stir continuously until the lentils emit a nutty aroma. Pour the tempered spices immediately on to the cucumber mixture. Allow to cool, then refrigerate until needed.

# warm okra salad

| | | | |
|---|---|---|---|
| 225 g (8 oz) | **okra** cut into medium slices | | **for the tempering** |
| | **oil for shallow frying** | 2 tsp | **oil** |
| 7 tbsp | **natural yoghurt** | $^1/_4$ tsp | **asafoetida** |
| | **salt** | 1 tsp | **mustard seeds** |
| | | 1 tsp | **cumin seeds** |
| | | 1 sprig | **curry leaves** (approx. 5–6 leaves) |
| | | 1 tsp | **urad dal** |
| | | 1 tsp | **chana dal** |
| | | 1 | **red chilli** cut into julienne strips |

**serves 4–6**   Heat some oil in a pan and shallow fry the okra until golden brown and crispy. Do this in batches, if necessary, in order not to overcrowd the pan. Remove and drain on kitchen paper.

Heat the oil for the tempering in a heavy frying pan. As soon as it starts to smoke, add the asafoetida, mustard seeds and cumin seeds. Allow the mustard seeds to sizzle and pop, then add the curry leaves. Continue to fry, stirring, for 30 seconds, then add the urad and chana dals, and sauté them until they turn golden and emit a nutty aroma. Add the chilli and stir for a few seconds, then pour into the yoghurt, mix thoroughly, and add salt to taste. Combine the yoghurt mixture and fried okra in a bowl. Serve either cold or at room temperature.

# spicy papaya salad

If you happen to come across a green papaya on your travels to your local Indian/Asian/Thai grocer, try this simple dish, which can be served as a sharper, healthier alternative to coleslaw.

| | | | |
|---|---|---|---|
| 1 | **green, unripe papaya** *peeled, de-seeded and coarsely grated* | | **for the tempering** |
| 1–2 tsp | **sugar** | 2 tbsp | **vegetable oil** |
| 1 tsp | **chilli powder** | 1 tsp | **asafoetida** |
| | **salt** | 2 tsp | **mustard seeds** |
| ½ | **lime** *juiced* | 2 tbsp | **peanuts** |

**serves 4–6**  Put the grated papaya into a bowl and add the sugar and chilli powder and enough lime juice to bring out the sharpness of the fruit. Season with salt to taste. Mix well.

Heat the oil in a heavy frying pan until it begins to smoke, then add the asafoetida and mustard seeds. As soon as they start to hiss and splutter, add the peanuts, sauté for a few seconds, then add to the papaya and mix thoroughly.

# beetroot raita

A refreshing dish that is a perfect accompaniment to a chicken or lamb biryani.

| | |
|---|---|
| 4 | **ready-cooked beetroots** *diced or grated* |
| 1 tsp | **ground cardamom** *plus extra for garnishing* |
| 2–3 tbsp | **fresh mint** *chopped* |
| 450 ml (16 fl oz) | **Greek yoghurt** |
| 1 tsp | **sugar** |
| 1 | **lemon** |
| | **salt** |

**serves 6**  Put the beetroot in a bowl and add the cardamom and 2 tablespoons of the chopped mint. In a separate bowl, whisk together the yoghurt with the sugar, a squeeze of lemon juice and salt to taste. Layer the beetroot and the yoghurt in a serving dish (a glass one would look pretty) and garnish with the remaining mint and a sprinkling of ground cardamom.

# cucumber raita

A true, classic raita, but the dill gives it an unusual lift which makes a perfect match for salmon in all its glorious forms.

| | |
|---:|:---|
| 1 | **cucumber** *washed and grated* |
| 450 ml (16 fl oz) | **natural yoghurt** |
| 4 tbsp | **dill** *finely chopped* |
| | **freshly ground black pepper** |
| 1 | **garlic clove** *crushed* |
| 1 tbsp | **vegetable oil** |
| $^1\!/_2$ tsp | **mustard seeds** |
| $^1\!/_2$ tsp | **cumin seeds** |
| pinch | **asafoetida** |
| 4–5 | **curry leaves** |

**serves 6**  Squeeze out any excess water from the grated cucumber and mix with the yoghurt. Stir in the dill, black pepper and garlic.

Heat the oil in a small frying pan. As soon as it starts to smoke, add the mustard seeds, cumin seeds, asafoetida and curry leaves, and fry, stirring, for 2–3 minutes, until fragrant. Pour on to the yoghurt and cucumber and stir through.

Leida's scrummy food served on banana leaves on the verandah in tiger territory. The last supper? Arriving at Leida's was like walking on to a film set for a location in paradise. The garden was fantastically lush with peppercorns and cardamoms growing wild. The scent is overwhelming and if you're a foodie, your mind instantly turns to wonderful dishes with ingredients picked from your own spice garden. Heaven if you live in London with no garden. Leida and her family prepared fish and chicken curries for me. The rice was prepared in the traditional way in a bamboo tube and cooked over an open fire. The romanticism of it was a little dented by the smoke, which made my eyes stream and nearly brought on an asthma attack. This was not helped by the news that we were in tiger territory and that **at any moment one of the 36 tigers might decide to drop by.**

# green and red chutneys

Two dips for the price of one! And an easy way to impress your guests. These are particularly versatile chutneys that go with most starters, plus they can be prepared well in advance and kept in the refrigerator for up to a week in airtight jars. If you want to make larger quantities, they can be kept frozen for up to three months – and, believe it or not, they retain their vibrant colour even after having been in the freezer.

The ingredients for the two chutneys are the same, you just add chilli and sugar to half the mixture to make the red version.

|  |  |  |  |
|---|---|---|---|
|  | **for both chutneys** | *1 tsp* | **for the red chutney** |
| 3 | **green chillies** | *2 tsp* | **red chilli powder** |
| *1 sprig* | **fresh mint leaves** | *2 tsp* | **sugar or fructose** |
| 3 | **garlic cloves** |  |  |
| *1 large* | **lemon** *skin and pips removed* |  |  |
| *1 bunch* | **fresh coriander leaves** *thick stalks removed* |  |  |
| *1 tsp* | **salt** |  |  |
| *75 ml (3 fl oz)* | **water** |  |  |

**makes 1 small bowl of each colour** Put all the ingredients except the chilli powder and sugar in a blender and process until you have a thick paste. Divide this mixture into two bowls. Leave one bowl untouched; this is the green chutney. To make the red chutney, which has a sweet/sour taste, add the chilli powder and sugar to the other bowl and mix well.

# coriander and walnut chutney

Ideal with Potato and Lamb Cutlets (page 31) or on its own with boiled rice.

| | |
|---|---|
| *225 g (8 oz)* | **fresh coriander leaves** |
| *10–12* | **hot green chillies** *de-seeded* |
| *2–3* | **garlic cloves** *peeled* |
| *25 g (1 oz)* | **walnuts** |
| *25 g (1 oz)* | **raisins** |
| *25 g (1 oz)* | **sugar** |
| *4* | **lemons** *juiced, or 6 tbsp white wine vinegar* |
| | **salt** |

**makes 1 bowl**  Roughly chop the coriander, chillies, garlic, walnuts and raisins, then put in a food processor and pulse a few times. Make sure the mixture does not turn into a paste. Dissolve the sugar in the lemon juice or vinegar, add to the coriander/walnut mixture, then season with salt to taste.

Sealed in an airtight container in the refrigerator, it will keep for up to a week.

# tamarind chutney

This is a very hot and spicy chutney, so use sparingly. It is used in the Tamarind Rice recipe (page 147), but also goes well with many other dishes, especially Potato and Lamb Cutlets (page 31), Chilli and Coriander Prawn Fritters (page 32) and the Lentil Dumplings (page 124). It will keep for two months or more in the refrigerator.

| | | | |
|---|---|---|---|
| 400 g (14 oz) | block wet tamarind | | for the masala powder |
| | salt | 2 tbsp | vegetable oil |
| 1/2 tsp | ground turmeric | 40 g (1 1/2 oz) | coriander seeds |
| 4 tbsp | palm sugar or jaggery | 6 | dried red chillies |
| | | 1/2 tsp | asafoetida |
| | | 1 tsp | whole black peppercorns |
| | | 1 tsp | cumin seeds |
| | | 1 tsp | fenugreek seeds |
| | | 1/2 tsp | mustard seeds |
| | | 1 tbsp | chana dal |
| | | 1 tbsp | urad dal |
| | | 1 sprig | curry leaves |

**makes about
200 g (7 oz)**

Soak the tamarind in 700 ml (1 1/4 pints) hot water for 15 minutes. Strain the tamarind water into a bowl, squeezing out as much liquid as possible from the tamarind pulp. Discard the pulp and set the tamarind water aside.

Heat the oil in a heavy frying pan. Add all the ingredients for the masala powder and sauté for 2–3 minutes. Allow the mixture to cool, then grind to a fine powder in a coffee grinder or pestle and mortar, and set aside.

Simmer the tamarind juice, salt, turmeric and palm sugar over a low heat until the mixture thickens to an almost jam-like consistency. Add the masala powder and mix thoroughly.

# carrot and apple pickle

This is the simplest of pickles to make and the most versatile. I have served it with Thai as well as Indian curries, but it can also be used to liven up any 'picklish' situation, such as a plate of cold meat or cheese.

| | | | | |
|---|---|---|---|---|
| 3 large | **Granny Smith apples** *washed* | | **for the tempering** | |
| 2 | **carrots** *cut into 5 cm (2 inch) julienne strips* | 240 ml (8 fl oz) | **vegetable oil** | |
| 10 | **green chillies** *slit in half lengthways* | 1 tsp | **mustard seeds** | |
| | | 1 tsp | **whole cumin seeds** | |
| | **for the apple marinade** | 1 large | **garlic clove** *crushed* | |
| 3 tsp | **red chilli powder** | 3 sprigs | **curry leaves** *(approx. 15 leaves)* | |
| 225 g (8 oz) | **sugar** | | | |
| 2 tsp | **ground cumin** | | | |
| 2 tbsp | **vegetable oil** | | | |
| | **salt** *to taste* | | | |

**makes 2 jars**  Place all the ingredients for the apple marinade in a large bowl, then cut the apples into wedges of about 2.5 cm (1 inch) and put them immediately into the mixture: this will prevent them from discolouring. Marinate for 10–15 minutes.

Heat the oil for the tempering in a wide pan until hot, add the mustard and cumin seeds and fry until they start to sizzle, then add the garlic and the curry leaves. Fry these for a few seconds, then add the carrots and chillies, coating well. Cook for 5–7 minutes until the carrots have softened slightly. Finally, add the marinated apples and continue to cook for a further 5 minutes. Allow the pickle to cool, then put into airtight containers or jars. Stored in the refrigerator, it will keep for 7–10 days.

# grenadine and orange dip

A wonderfully vibrant, sunset-coloured dip, reminiscent of cocktails in the Caribbean. A perfect complement to Duck Samosas (page 34).

| | |
|---:|:---|
| 3 | **oranges** *juiced* |
| 1 | **lime** *juiced* |
| 100 ml (3 1/2 fl oz) | **grenadine syrup** |
| 4–5 | **cloves** |
| 2 x 2.5 cm (1 inch) | **cinnamon sticks** |
| 1 | **whole star anise** |
| 1 small | **green chilli** *sliced and de-seeded* |

**serves 4–6**   Heat the orange juice, lime juice and grenadine in a non-stick saucepan. Add the cloves, cinnamon and star anise, bring to the boil, then lower the heat and simmer until the liquid has reduced to a jam-like consistency. Add the chilli to the pan at the end, to give the flavour a sharp kick. Allow to cool before serving.

At last, a chance to languish on a lagoon. We were on lake Vembanad in Cochin on the Malabar coast, which leads out to the Arabian Sea. Chef Rashid prepared a breakfast banquet for me that was worth getting up for. The Chinese influence is obvious from the hat, which my director, Janice, bought for me. Whether it suits me is for you to decide. If the answer's no, don't tell me.

# tomato and chive dip

A dip with a pronounced kick, which goes exceedingly well with Crab Samosas (page 36).

| | | | | |
|---|---|---|---|---|
| 1 tbsp | **vegetable oil** | | 1/4 tsp | **ground turmeric** |
| 3 | **whole cloves** | | 1/4 tsp | **ground cumin** |
| 1 large | **black cardamom** | | 3 tsp | **chilli powder** |
| 3 | **green cardamoms** | | | **salt** |
| 1 x 5 cm (2 inch) | **cinnamon stick** | | 1 tbsp | **tomato ketchup** |
| 1–2 | **garlic cloves** crushed | | 1 tbsp | **cider vinegar** |
| 1 x 2.5 cm (1 inch) piece | **fresh ginger** finely grated | | 1 tsp | **chopped fresh chives** |
| 1 x 400 g (14 oz) | **can chopped tomatoes** | | | |

**serves 6–8**    Heat the oil in a saucepan, then add the cloves, black cardamom, green cardamoms, and cinnamon. After a minute, add the garlic and ginger and cook for a further 1–2 minutes. Add the tomatoes, turmeric, cumin and chilli powder and continue to cook for 15–20 minutes. Remove from the heat, allow to cool slightly, then process until smooth in a food processor or blender. Add salt to taste. Strain through a fine sieve and return to the pan. Add the ketchup and cider vinegar, bring to the boil, then lower the heat and simmer until slightly reduced. Allow to cool, then add the chives.

# aubergine relish *(Baingan Bharta)*

This is similar to the Middle Eastern baba ganoush, otherwise known as aubergine caviar. It's ideal as a snack with pitta or any flat bread.

| | |
|---|---|
| 2 medium | **aubergines** *weighing about 700 g (1 ¼ lb)* |
| 1 tsp | **cumin seeds** *freshly roasted and ground* |
| 50 ml (2 fl oz) | **vegetable oil** |
| 2 medium | **onions** *finely sliced* |
| | **salt** |
| 2 | **garlic cloves** *finely chopped* |
| 1 | **green chilli** *finely chopped* |
| 2 dsp | **tamarind paste or lemon juice** |
| 2 tbsp | **natural yoghurt** |
| 1 tbsp | **fresh mint** *finely chopped* |

**serves 4**   Place the whole aubergines under the grill and cook them until their skin becomes crispy. Turn them occasionally so that all the sides brown evenly and the aubergines cook inside. Allow to cool in a bowl covered in clingfilm. Remove the skin and mash the flesh to a pulp. Add the cumin.

Heat the oil in a frying pan, add the sliced onions with a pinch of salt, and fry until golden brown. Remove with a slotted spoon and put to one side. In the same pan, fry the garlic for 1 minute, then add the chilli, along with the mashed aubergines, and stir vigorously. Add the tamarind paste or lemon juice and the fried onions. Fold in the yoghurt and cook for a further minute. Remove from the heat and allow to cool. Serve in a bowl garnished with the mint.

# Pillau talk!

Imagine Britain without chips, France without garlic, Poland without cabbage, Ant without Dec. Get the picture? Needless to say, rice is one of the main building blocks of Indian food (and just about every other Asian cuisine).

Each culture has its own preference in terms of the variety of rice and its preparation. There are many different types of rice in India, but here I have used only basmati, since it is widely available and is virtually foolproof. Traditionally, basmati was only used for biryanis and on special occasions, because it was too expensive for daily use. Now that it's cultivated throughout Asia, and in the US, its use is widespread. The Moguls, who came from Persia, brought with them traditional rice dishes that were incorporated into Indian cuisine, such as biryanis and pillaus. Incidentally, rice flour is used to make breads, sweet dishes and snacks.

I've included eight rice dishes because eight is the cosmic number of an ancient sanskrit text and it is a complete yet infinite number. That, and I couldn't think of any more. (Actually, I made that up.) Some of the recipes are meals in themselves, others complement main courses. I haven't included a recipe for plain boiled rice because everyone has their own favourite method. If you haven't found yours yet, follow the one given for Tamarind Rice (page 147).

# RICE DISHES

# rice with caramelised onions and pine nuts *(Chilgoza Rice)*

A subtle-flavoured, fragrant rice, which is a wonderful accompaniment to Chicken Dhansak (page 82), Meatballs in a Green Sauce (page 102) and or any game dishes. If you're out to impress your guests, this rice will do the trick. And you don't need to spend an age slaving over the cooker to make it.

| | |
|---|---|
| 400 g (14 oz) | **basmati rice** *washed in lukewarm water to remove starch and left in cold water to soak* |
| 2 tbsp | **ghee or vegetable oil** |
| 50 g (2 oz) | **pine nuts** |
| 4 | **cardamom pods** |
| 2–3 | **cinnamon sticks** |
| 3 tsp | **salt** *according to taste* |
| 1 medium | **onion** *finely sliced* |
| 700 ml ( 1¼ pints) | **hot water** |
| 1 tsp | **sugar** |

**serves 4–6**   Heat the ghee in a wide, heavy-bottomed saucepan. As soon as it starts to smoke, add the pine nuts and fry them until they turn golden brown. Remove with a slotted spoon, drain on kitchen paper and put to one side. To the same oil, add the cardamom pods, cinnamon sticks and a pinch of salt. Add the onions and sauté them until they caramelise and are golden brown in colour.

Drain and rinse the rice in cold water, then add to the pan and stir to mix. Pour in the water, add the sugar and remaining salt, and cook until most of the liquid has evaporated and small craters form on the surface of the rice. Reduce the heat as low as possible, place a clean dry cloth over the mouth of the saucepan and cover firmly with a lid. If possible, place a heavy weight on top of the lid, to enable the maximum amount of steam to build up inside the saucepan. Leave the rice on the heat for 10–15 minutes, then test to see if it is done by taking a grain and biting it with your teeth. If necessary, continue to cook for a further 5 minutes. Turn out the rice on to a serving dish and sprinkle with the pine nuts.

# tamarind rice

A typical, South Indian dish, great for taking on outings and picnics, or travelling with in a tiffi[n]
bit of bad news: it does take a while to prepare, but, by Jove, it packs a punch. If it's too spicy, add [?]
raisins to give a bit of sweetness. Serve with a helping of natural yoghurt.

| | |
|---|---|
| 400 g (14 oz) | **basmati rice** *rinsed and soaked in water for 20 minutes* |
| | **salt** |
| 1 tsp | **ground turmeric** |
| 2 tbsp | **sesame oil** |
| 50 g (2 oz) | **roasted peanuts** |
| 3 tbsp | **Tamarind Chutney** *(see page 138)* |

**for the tempering**

| | |
|---|---|
| 1 tbsp | **vegetable oil** |
| 2 tsp | **mustard seeds** |
| 1 tbsp | **chana dal** *washed and rinsed* |
| 1 tbsp | **urad dal** *washed and rinsed* |
| 1 tsp | **asafoetida** |
| 4–6 | **curry leaves** |

**for the garnish powder**

| | |
|---|---|
| 1 tbsp | **sesame seeds** |
| 1 tbsp | **desiccated coconut** |

**serves 4–6** First make the garnish powder by dry roasting the sesame seeds and coconut in a small pan for 5 minutes or until golden. Allow to cool, then grind to a fine powder in either a blender or pestle and mortar.

Bring 700 ml (1¼ pints) of water to the boil in a heavy-bottomed saucepan with 1–2 teaspoons of salt and the turmeric. Drain the rice, add it to the pan and cook until most of the liquid has evaporated and small craters have formed on the surface. Lower the heat to minimum, place a clean, dry cloth over the mouth of the saucepan, cover firmly with a lid, and leave for 10–15 minutes. Once the rice is cooked, spoon it on to a platter, allow to cool, then drizzle over the sesame oil.

Heat the vegetable oil in a small pan and, as soon as it starts to smoke, add the mustard seeds, both types of dal, the asafoetida and curry leaves. When the mixture starts to splutter, add the roasted peanuts and sauté for 2–3 minutes. Pour over the rice, add the tamarind chutney and garnish powder, and stir thoroughly.

# ginger rice

...ind it may well be effective as one. If it is, that's a bonus. I like it
...atic side dish that's the perfect accompaniment for many fish and
...alls in a Green Sauce (page 102).

| | | | for the tempering |
|---|---|---|---|
| | *plus zest of 1* | 1 tbsp | **ghee** |
| 2.5 cm (1 inch) piece | **fresh ginger** *finely sliced into julienne strips* | pinch | **asafoetida** |
| | **salt** | $\frac{1}{2}$ tsp | **mustard seeds** |
| 1 tsp | **ghee** | 1 tsp | **chana dal** |
| pinch | **turmeric** | 1 tsp | **urad dal** |
| | | 1 sprig | **curry leaves** |
| | | 2 | **green chillies** *slit in half lengthways* |

**serves 4–6**   Wash the rice in hot water, rinse it several times in cold water to remove as much starch as
possible, then soak in cold water, with some salt, for at least 30 minutes. Drain.

Combine 700 ml ($1\frac{1}{4}$ pints) water, the lemon juice and zest, half the ginger, some salt and
the ghee in a large, heavy-bottomed saucepan and bring to the boil. Allow the ginger to soften
slightly, then add the rice and turmeric, and stir to mix. Cook the rice until most of the liquid has
evaporated and small craters appear on the surface. Lower the heat immediately to minimum.
Place a clean dry cloth over the mouth of the saucepan and cover with the lid. Leave to simmer for
at least 10 minutes, then remove from the heat. Do not lift the lid during this time.

Heat the ghee in a shallow frying pan. As soon as it begins to smoke, add the asafoetida and
the remaining ginger, and stir-fry for a few seconds, then add the mustard seeds and allow them to
pop and crackle. Add the two dals and continue to stir-fry until they become golden. Finally, add
the curry leaves and chillies. Lift the lid off the rice pan, pour the tempered mixture on to the rice,
then replace the lid for a minute or two before stirring the tempering mixture into the rice with a
fork.

A post-prandial puff?

# lentil pillau *(Khichdi)*

Aromatic Indian spices add a delicious fragrance to this simple, but tasty, lentil pillau, which is ideal with fish and natural yoghurt. It is often eaten when someone is feeling a bit under the weather, as it is gentle on the stomach, and is therefore perfect for anyone recovering from an illness.

| | |
|---:|:---|
| 2 tbsp | **ghee** |
| 1 tsp | **cumin seeds** |
| 2 | **onions** *sliced* |
| 3–4 | **black cardamoms** |
| 3–4 | **cloves** |
| 2–3 x 5 cm (2 inch) | **cinnamon sticks** |
| | **salt** |
| 2 | **garlic cloves** *crushed* |
| 2.5 cm (1 inch) piece | **fresh ginger** *grated* |
| 150 g (5 $^1$/$_2$ oz) | **moong dal** *soaked in water for 30 minutes* |
| 400 g (14 oz) | **basmati rice** *rinsed and soaked in water for 20 minutes* |

**serves 4–6**  Heat a heavy-based saucepan until hot. Add the ghee, cumin seeds, onions, black cardamoms, cloves and cinnamon, and fry, stirring occasionally, until the onions have turned golden; about 10 minutes. Add a pinch of salt, the garlic and ginger, and mix well. Drain the lentils and add to the pan with about 50 ml (2 fl oz) water, then reduce the heat, cover with a lid, and simmer for 10 minutes, stirring from time to time, until the lentils soften. If the mixture becomes too dry, add a little bit more water.

Drain the rice and add to the lentils, along with 850 ml (1 $^1$/$_2$ pints) hot water and 2 teaspoons salt. Bring to the boil and cook the rice until most of the liquid has evaporated and small craters form on the surface. Lower the heat to minimum, cover with a clean, dry cloth and a tightly fitting lid, and leave for 15–20 minutes until all the water has been absorbed and the rice is tender.

# chicken and prune biryani

During filming for *A Place in France*, I prepared this meal for the our first honeymoon couple, chiefly to distract them from the numerous shortcomings of the B&B at the time. I pulled out all the stops, along with my seven veils, and produced this lavish biryani. By the end of the meal, they had both proposed to me!

| | | | | |
|---|---|---|---|---|
| 5 | **chicken breasts** *each cut into four pieces* | | 100 g (3½ oz) | **dried prunes** *stoned* |
| 450 g (1 lb) | **natural yoghurt** | | 450 g (1 lb) | **basmati rice** |
| 6 | **onions** *sliced and fried until golden* | | 2 | **black cardamoms** |
| 4 | **garlic cloves** *crushed* | | 6 | **green cardamoms** |
| 50 g (2 oz) | **fresh ginger** *finely grated* | | 2 x 5 cm (2 inch) | **cinnamon sticks** |
| 4 | **green chillies** | | 4 | **cloves** |
| bunch | **fresh coriander** *stalks and leaves separated* | | 2 | **bay leaves** |
| | **salt** | | 200 g (7 oz) | **Puy lentils** *cooked* |
| 1 generous tsp | **garam masala** | | 150 g (5½ oz) | **butter** |
| 3 | **oranges** | | | |

**serves 6**  Blend the yoghurt, half the fried onion, the garlic, ginger, chillies, coriander stalks, salt and garam masala in a food processor until smooth. Combine with the chicken in a bowl, cover and leave to marinate in the refrigerator for at least 2 hours, or overnight if you prefer.

Grate the zest of two of the oranges and put to one side. Squeeze the juice from all three oranges into a bowl, add half the zest and the prunes. Leave the prunes to marinate for at least an hour (more won't hurt), then drain them, reserving the liquid.

Cook the chicken by simmering it gently with the marinade in a non-stick pan for about 15 minutes until just tender, then leave to cool. Wash the rice in several changes of cold water and soak it in salted water for half an hour. Bring a large pan of water to the boil. Add the cardamoms, cinnamon, cloves, bay leaves and some of the chopped coriander leaves. Drain the rice, add it to the boiling water; salt to taste. When the water returns to the boil, cook for 2 minutes, then drain and mix with the remaining orange zest and Puy lentils. In the same hot pan you used to cook the rice, melt the butter, add a layer of half the rice mixture, then a layer of half the remaining fried onions, then half the prunes. Add all the chicken in one layer, then cover with a layer of the remaining rice, then the prunes, and finishing with the fried onions. Pour over the reserved orange-prune juice. Cover the pan with a lid and cook on a high heat for 5 minutes, then reduce the heat to low and leave for 40 minutes. To serve, turn out the contents of the pan on to a large, flat dish. The crusty layer at the bottom of the pan is a delicacy and should be served around the edges.

My version of Cleopatra's barge on a budget. These rice boats were introduced into Kerala by the Chinese. I bet you're expecting me to make some terrible joke about a load of old junk, but I'm going to resist. I must say that when I imagined myself cooking on a boat, I was thinking along the lines of a glamorous six-deck yacht with a helipad, so when this came gliding into view I thought it was just for my luggage. Did I go into Diva mode? As you can see, to no avail.

# minced lamb and lentil pillau *(Masour Pillau)*

An economical recipe that makes a little lamb go a long way. It is an easy, one-pot dinner-party dish.

| | | | |
|---|---|---|---|
| 450 g (1 lb) | **minced lamb** | 3 tsp | **salt** |
| 600 g (1¼ lb) | **basmati rice** | 1 tsp | **saffron strands** *soaked in 200ml* |
| 50 g (2 oz) | **Puy lentils** *washed and drained* | | *(7 fl oz) hot water for 10–15 minutes* |
| | **vegetable oil for frying** | | |
| 4 large | **onions** *sliced* | | **spices for the rice** |
| 2 | **garlic cloves** *crushed* | 1 tsp | **black peppercorns** |
| 5 cm (2 inch) piece | **fresh ginger** *grated* | 3 x 5 cm (2 inch) | **cinnamon sticks** |
| 2 medium | **tomatoes** | 3 | **cloves** |
| 2 | **green chillies** *slit in half lengthways* | 3 | **cardamoms** |
| 1 tsp | **ground cumin** | 65 g (2¾ oz) | **butter** |
| 1 tsp | **garam masala** | | |
| 1 tsp | **red chilli powder** | | **for the garnish** |
| ½ tsp | **saffron strands** | 6 | **quail's eggs** *or 3 hen's eggs, hard-* |
| 1 tbsp | **natural yoghurt** | | *boiled until the yolks are just set* |
| 3–4 sprigs | **mint** *chopped* | | **fresh coriander** *chopped* |

**serves 6–8** Wash the rice and leave it to soak in cold water while preparing the other ingredients. Place the lentils in a saucepan with 400 ml (14 fl oz) water, bring to the boil, then lower the heat and simmer for 30–45 minutes until tender. If the pan becomes too dry, add more hot water.

Heat the oil in a frying pan and, as soon as it smokes, add half the onion and fry until golden brown and crisp. Remove with a slotted spoon, drain on kitchen paper and set aside. Add the remaining onion to the pan, and fry until caramelised. Stir in the garlic and ginger, then the tomatoes, chillies, ground cumin, garam masala, chilli powder and saffron strands. Add the lamb, and cook, continuing to stir, for 15 minutes. When most of the liquid has evaporated, add the yoghurt, then leave to simmer for a further 15 minutes. Stir in the mint and remove from the heat.

In a separate, large pan, bring 1.5 litres (2½ pints) water to the boil. Once it reaches a rolling boil, add the drained rice, salt, all the whole spices and a drizzle of oil to keep the grains separate. Cook for 3–5 minutes, then strain the rice and leave to stand. Using the same pan, melt the butter and cover the base with a layer of cooked rice. Add a layer of the reserved fried onions, then a layer of lentils, then pour in some saffron water. Cover with a thin layer of rice and some of the cooked mince. Repeat, finishing with a layer of onions. Cover with a clean, dry, cloth then steam on a low heat for 15–20 minutes. Turn out on to a large dish and garnish.

# Hyderabadi spring lamb biryani

What makes this dish so special is that, unlike most biryanis, the lamb and rice are cooked together from the start. First, though, the lamb is marinated for several hours, the green papaya and yoghurt being natural tenderisers. It is essential, too, that you use the best, leanest, youngest meat. Mutton dressed as lamb will not do.

It's best to marinate the lamb overnight in the refrigerator and then cook it the next day. Make sure, however, that you have everything ready to hand before you start cooking the rice, as you need to assemble the layers quickly, while the rice is still hot.

| | | | |
|---|---|---|---|
| 1 kg (2 ¹/₄ lb) | **lean spring lamb** preferably leg, cut into 5 cm (2 inch) cubes, plus bones, if available | | **for the rice** |
| | | 800 g (1 ³/₄ lb) | **basmati rice** |
| | | ¹/₂ tsp | **black cumin seeds** (kala jeera) |
| | **for the tenderising mix** | 4 | **cloves** |
| 3 tbsp | **green papaya** finely grated | 3–4 large | **black cardamoms** |
| 2 tbsp | **ginger** finely grated | 8–10 | **black peppercorns** |
| 4–6 | **garlic cloves** crushed | 2 x 5 cm (2 inch) | **cinnamon sticks** |
| | | 2 | **bay leaves** |
| | **for the marinade** | ¹/₂ tsp | **ground nutmeg** |
| 350 ml (12 fl oz) | **vegetable oil** | 1 tbsp | **fresh coriander** finely chopped |
| 2 medium | **onions** sliced and fried to a golden brown | 2–4 | **green chillies** finely chopped |
| 250 ml (9 fl oz) | **natural yoghurt** | 4 tsp | **salt** to taste (generally 1 tsp to 1 cup of rice) |
| 1 tbsp | **fresh mint** finely chopped | | |
| 3–4 | **green chillies** finely chopped | | **for the biryani layers** |
| 1 tbsp | **fresh coriander** finely chopped | 225 g (8 oz) | **ghee** |
| 1 tsp | **garam masala** | 1 tsp | **saffron strands** soaked in 125 ml (4 fl oz) milk for 30 minutes |
| 1 tsp | **ground turmeric** | | |
| 1–2 tsp | **red chilli powder** according to taste | 1 | **lemon** juiced |
| 1 ¹/₂ tsp | **salt** to taste | 1 tbsp | **fresh coriander** chopped |
| | | 1 tbsp | **fresh mint** finely chopped |
| | | 1 tbsp | **green chillies** chopped |
| | | 2–3 medium | **onions** sliced and fried until golden brown |
| | | 350 ml (12 fl oz) | **vegetable oil** |

**for the garnish** *any combination of the following:*

**more fried onions**

**fresh coriander or mint** *chopped*

**almonds or pine nuts** *toasted*

**sprinkling of rosewater**

**hard-boiled eggs** *quartered*

**raisins**

**serves 6–8**    Rub the tenderising mix into the lamb, together with the bones, if you have them, then cover and leave for 1–2 hours. Meanwhile, heat the oil for the marinade in a non-stick frying pan, add the onions and a pinch of salt, and fry until golden brown. Remove with a slotted spoon, drain on kitchen paper, allow to cool, and reserve one third for the garnish. Blend to a paste in a food processor or blender. Put in a bowl, add the remaining marinade ingredients, followed by the lamb, cover, and leave for a minimum of 2–3 hours, or overnight in the refrigerator.

Wash the rice, then leave to soak in warm water for 1–2 hours while preparing the ingredients for the biryani layers: fry your onions in the oil, chop your herbs and chillies, soak your saffron and juice your lemon. Having done so, bring a large saucepan containing 3 litres (5$\frac{1}{4}$ pints) water to the boil, add the drained rice, plus all the other rice ingredients, and bring back to the boil. Cook for 1–2 minutes, then strain the rice through a colander.

Using the same large saucepan, melt the ghee and put in the lamb with all its marinade. Add a layer of half the cooked rice, sprinkle over half the lemon juice, some of the chopped coriander and mint, and half the reserved fried onions. Pour over half the saffron milk. Now add the rest of the rice and repeat the additions of lemon juice, mint, coriander, saffron milk and fried onions. Place a clean, damp cloth over the mouth of the saucepan and close firmly with a lid. If possible, put a heavy weight on top of the lid, to seal it. Turn the heat to high and cook until enough steam has built up inside the saucepan for some to seep out under the lid. Lower the heat to medium and cook for 5–10 minutes, then reduce to low and continue to cook for about 1 hour 20 minutes. Do not at any time open the lid, as this will release the steam that has built up inside.

When the cooking time is completed, remove the lid and insert a knife into the biryani to check if the meat has cooked through. If it's not completely tender, cook for a further 10–15 minutes, once more sealing the pan. Leave the biryani to stand for 15 minutes, then turn out on to a large serving platter, piling it up in the centre. Garnish with the remaining reserved fried onions and whatever else takes your fancy.

# fish biryani

When I was filming in Kerala, I stayed in a magnificent dwelling in Tellicherry overlooking the Arabian Sea. My hostess, Faiza, treated me to a delicious fish biryani, a local speciality of the Mopla Muslim community. I felt, though, that it could do with a 'Rezaring'. I simply adjusted the cooking time of the fish by first sealing it in the pan and allowing it to marinate in the sauce for a longer period. In this way it could absorb maximum flavour before it was layered in the rice.

It makes a stunning dinner-party showpiece and my suggestion to you is to serve it with the Warm Okra Salad (page 130) or the Spicy Papaya Salad (page 131). So have fun and do try this dish, it is absolutely delicious. I served it one afternoon at my sister's and even the children, who are averse to fish, were converted.

| | | | |
|---|---|---|---|
| 450 g (1 lb) | **king fish, haddock, hake or any firm white fish** *skinned and filleted* | $^1/_2$ tsp | **chilli powder** |
| | **vegetable oil for shallow frying** | $^1/_2$ tsp | **ground turmeric** |
| | | | **for the crisp onion mixture** |
| | **for the spice coating** | 4 | **onions** *thinly sliced* |
| 1 tbsp | **chilli powder** | 100 g (3 $^1/_2$ oz) | **pine nuts** |
| $^1/_2$ tsp | **ground turmeric** | 2 tbsp | **raisins** |
| 2 tsp | **garam masala** | | **vegetable oil for deep frying** |
| $^1/_2$ tsp | **salt** | | |
| | | | **for the rice mixture** |
| | **for the masala** | 25 g (1 oz) | **ghee** *plus 1 tbsp* |
| 25 g (1 oz) | **ghee** | 3 | **cardamom pods** |
| 2 | **cardamoms** | 3 | **cloves** |
| 2 | **cloves** | 2 x 3 cm (1 $^1/_2$ inch) | **cinnamon sticks** |
| 3 cm (1 $^1/_4$ inch) | **cinnamon stick** | 2 | **garlic cloves** *finely chopped* |
| 2 | **garlic cloves** *chopped* | 3 cm (1 $^1/_2$ inch) piece | **fresh ginger** *finely chopped* |
| 25 g (1 oz) | **fresh ginger** *shredded* | 2 tbsp | **fresh mint** *chopped* |
| 3 | **green chillies** *chopped* | 2 | **green chillies** *chopped* |
| 3 tbsp | **fresh coriander** *chopped* | 2 tbsp | **fresh coriander** *chopped* |
| 2 tbsp | **fresh mint** *chopped* | 450 g (1 lb) | **basmati rice** *rinsed and soaked in cold water for 15 minutes* |
| 4 | **red onions** *roughly chopped* | | |
| 2 | **tomatoes** *chopped* | | |
| 1 tbsp | **ground coriander** | | |

**for finishing**

*generous pinch*   **saffron strands** *soaked in 4 tbsp warm water for 1 hour*

*few drops*   **rosewater**

**serves 4–6**   Cut the fish into thick slices. Combine the chilli powder, turmeric, garam masala and salt in a small bowl, add enough water to moisten (about 2 tablespoons) and rub this spice coating over each piece of fish.

Heat a little oil in a frying pan and seal the fish on both sides. Try not to overcook; 1 minute either side is sufficient. Remove the fish from the pan and set aside on kitchen paper while you make the sauce.

Heat the ghee in a large saucepan and toss in the cardamoms, cloves and cinnamon. After a few seconds, add the garlic, ginger and chillies and fry for about 2–3 minutes, then add the coriander and mint. Tip in the onions and fry until golden. Add the tomatoes, followed by the ground coriander, chilli powder and turmeric, and stir and fry for a minute or so. Pour in 350 ml (12 fl oz) water, and cook the sauce over a moderate-to-low heat until it thickens. This should take 20–30 minutes. Add the fish and coat with the sauce. Cover the pan, remove from the heat, and leave to one side for 10 minutes so that the fish can absorb the spicy flavours.

Deep-fry the sliced onions in hot oil until they are crisp, then drain on kitchen paper. In another pan, fry the pine nuts in a couple of tablespoons of the same oil until golden, then add to the onions along with the raisins. Leave this mixture to one side while you make the rice.

For the rice heat the ghee in a large saucepan, toss in the cardamoms, cloves and cinnamon, and swirl them around for a moment or two before adding the garlic, ginger, mint, chillies and coriander. Add the drained rice to the pan and stir and fry for 2 minutes over a low heat. Pour in 1 litre (1³⁄₄ pints) boiling water and simmer for about 10 minutes until the rice has absorbed most of the water. The grains should be fluffy and separate. Strain through a colander.

Add a generous tablespoon of ghee to the same pan in which you cooked the rice. Add a layer of half the cooked rice, spread with a third of the crisp onion mixture and sprinkle with a couple of teaspoons of saffron water. Place the fish and sauce on top, then cover with the rest of the rice, followed by another third of the onion mixture (saving the rest for the garnish) and sprinkle with the remaining saffron water. Cover the pan with a tight-fitting lid and simmer on a very low heat for 10–15 minutes. Use a heat diffuser if you have one.

After this time, the fish should be just cooked through. Spoon the rice on to a serving plate and arrange the fish on top. Garnish with the remaining crisp onion mixture, sprinkle with a few drops of rosewater, then serve.

One thing the **Indians and British have in common is that we both have a very sweet tooth**. And although it could get me into trouble, I think many Indian desserts are rather too sweet. Consequently, the recipes included here are my favourites either because they take me back to my childhood or because they're not overpoweringly sugary.

Generally, desserts are not made every day in Indian households. They tend to be served mainly on special occasions such as weddings, religious festivals or for entertaining guests. Personally, I think you should eat them as the mood takes you.

# DESSERTS

# Indian rice pudding

This is an Indian variation on the classic British rice pudding. Or maybe it's the other way round. Who knows? Who cares? It's delicious.

| | |
|---:|:---|
| 100 g (3 1/2 oz) | **basmati rice** |
| 1 litre (1 3/4 pints) | **whole milk** |
| 300 ml (1/2 pint) | **single cream** |
| few pinches | **ground cardamom** |
| 3–4 tbsp | **sugar** |
| 1 tbsp | **rosewater** |

**serves 4–6**  Wash the rice in water, place in a bowl, cover with hot water and set aside to soak for 10 minutes. Drain the rice and place in a heavy-bottomed saucepan. Stir in the milk, cream, cardamom and sugar, and bring to the boil. Taste and sweeten with more sugar if required. Lower the heat, and simmer for 20 minutes until you get a rich, creamy texture. Add the rosewater, simmer for a further few minutes, then serve.

# strained sweetened yoghurt *(Shrikand)*

A traditional Indian dessert, wickedly luscious with Pooris (page 39).

| | |
|---|---|
| *450 g (1 lb)* | **Greek yoghurt** |
| *pinch* | **saffron strands** *soaked in 1 tbsp milk for 30 minutes* |
| *2 tbsp* | **caster sugar, or more to taste** |
| *¹/₄ tsp* | **ground cardamom** |
| *1 tsp* | **ground almonds (optional)** |
| *1 tsp* | **slivered almonds** |
| *1 tsp* | **pistachios** *coarsely chopped* |

**serves 4** Suspend the yoghurt in a piece of muslin set over a bowl for 2–3 hours, to drain off all the whey.

Tip the drained yoghurt from the cloth into a bowl and stir in the saffron milk. Add the sugar, whisk until it is the consistency of whipped cream, then sprinkle in the cardamom and ground almonds, if using. Spoon equal amounts into four small ramekin dishes and garnish with the slivered almonds and pistachios. Leave to set in the refrigerator for 1 hour, then serve.

Nigel's always been great with kids. He decided to go back to nature, though I thought this was taking things a little too far. He wanted me to milk Elizabeth. I told him I would only do it if I could use the milk for my bath. That soon set him straight and as you can see he's simply in his element. I helped by holding on to her horns. More I could not bring myself to do.

# sweet vermicelli cooked in milk *(Sheer Khurma)*

A traditional dish served on the Muslim festival of Eid. The vermicelli (sivayyan) is covered with subtle spices, almonds and pistachios, and floats in a delicious, saffron-flavoured milk. For a dessert with such delicate, unique flavours, it is very quick to prepare. It will keep for 3 days in the refrigerator and can also be frozen for 2 months. Make sure you defrost completely in the refrigerator overnight before reheating.

| | |
|---|---|
| *2.25 litres (4 pints)* | **whole milk** |
| *175 ml (6 fl oz)* | **single cream** |
| *2 tbsp* | **ghee** |
| *50 g (2 oz)* | **dry vermicelli** *broken into 2.5–5 cm (1–2 inch) lengths* |
| *1 tbsp* | **slivered almonds** |
| *2 tbsp* | **slivered pistachios** |
| *1 tbsp* | **charuli** *boiled and skins removed (optional) see notes on ingredients* |
| *2 generous pinches* | **saffron strands** |
| | **salt** |
| *1 tsp* | **ground cardamom** |
| *1 tsp* | **ground nutmeg** |
| *115 g (4 oz)* | **caster sugar** |
| *1 tbsp* | **sultanas** *soaked in warm water* |

**serves 6–8**   Pour the milk and cream into a heavy-bottomed saucepan, bring gently to the boil and leave to simmer while you prepare the vermicelli.

Melt the ghee in a separate, deep, heavy-bottomed saucepan set over a low heat. Add the vermicelli and sauté until golden brown. Now add the slivered almonds, pistachios and charuli, and continue to sauté for 5–10 minutes, until the nuts take on a light golden hue.

Add the saffron, a pinch of salt and the heated milk mixture to the vermicelli and bring to the boil, then lower the heat and cook for 10–15 minutes. The longer the milk is allowed to cook, the thicker and more concentrated it will become.

Add the cardamom, nutmeg and sugar, and stir until the sugar dissolves. Now add the drained sultanas and leave to simmer for a further 15–20 minutes, stirring occasionally. The Sheer Khurma is ready once the vermicelli has softened and become translucent, the nuts and saffron strands have floated to the surface, and a thin film of ghee has risen to the top. Serve hot, warm or cold, according to preference, ladled into deep bowls.

# China grass

Yes, you're right. This is a very silly name for a pudding. I included it because I wanted to confuse you. In case you're interested, China grass is another name for agar agar, which is available from Asian grocers. The pudding itself is similar to the Italian panacotta.

| | |
|---:|:---|
| 300ml (10 fl oz) | **double cream** |
| 4 tbsp | **sugar** or to taste |
| 500 ml (17 fl oz) | **whole milk** |
| 2 tbsp | **agar agar flakes** |
| 2 pinches | **ground cardamom** |
| 2 pinches | **ground nutmeg** |
| 2 pinches | **saffron strands** |
| 2 tsp | **almonds** slivered (optional) |
| 2 tsp | **pistachios** slivered (optional) |

**serves 4**   Put the double cream, the sugar and the milk into a saucepan. Sprinkle over the agar agar flakes evenly on the surface of the liquid. Place on the heat and bring to the boil – avoid stirring as this will prevent you from assessing whether the flakes have dissolved or not. Simmer for 10 minutes or so on a medium-to-low heat, stirring occasionally until the flakes have disappeared from the liquid. It is important that you cook the mixture until the agar agar flakes are fully dissolved or the China grass will not set. Now boil the mixture fairly hard for 1 minute, being careful not to cause the contents of the pan to overflow. Remove the pan from the heat and add a pinch of cardamom and nutmeg.

Pour the mixture into a shallow Pyrex dish or into individual moulds. Sprinkle on the rest of the cardamom and nutmeg with the saffron and the nuts (if using). Allow the mixture to cool at room temperature and then put in the refrigerator until set, which takes up to $1^{1}/_{2}$ hours. To serve, cut the set mixture into diamond shapes, or serve in the individual moulds.

# crème caramel

As a child, I always yearned for crème caramel, but my mother has a problem with any dessert made with eggs, as she hates the smell of them raw. The only way she could contemplate making it for me was by adding cardamom and saffron to mask the smell. She has been making this version for years, and it has become a firm family favourite.

You will need to make it the day before, as it must set overnight in the refrigerator. If you are given to bouts of depression or suicidal tendencies, do not on any account attempt to turn out this pudding. Rest assured, it will taste the same whether the caramel is on the top or the bottom.

| | | |
|---|---|---|
| 700 ml (1 ¼ pints) | **whole milk** | **for the caramel** |
| 6 | **eggs** | 3 heaped tbsp  **sugar** |
| 225 g (8 oz) | **caster sugar** | |
| 1 tsp | **ground cardamom** | |
| 1 tsp | **ground nutmeg** | |
| pinch | **saffron** | |
| 250 ml (8 fl oz) | **single cream** | |

**serves 8–10**   Preheat the oven to 170°–180°C/32°–35°F/Gas Mark 3–4.

Place all the ingredients except for the cream, and sugar for the caramel, in a blender and process until the sugar has dissolved. Alternatively, whisk everything together by hand. Stir in the cream.

Melt the sugar in a saucepan, then cook it until it caramelises and turns a deep chestnut brown. Pour immediately into an ovenproof dish just large enough to hold the custard and leave the caramel to set. If the mixture comes to the top of the dish it will be easier to turn out. Pour over the custard mixture, place in the oven and bake for 30–45 minutes. Test to see if the pudding has set by inserting a flat knife into the centre of the dish. If it comes away clean, the pudding can be removed from the oven. Allow to cool, then leave to set in the refrigerator overnight. Just prior to serving, turn out the pudding into a dish so that the caramel is on top.

# lychee and almond kulfi

This is a light, egg-free Indian ice-cream, truly refreshing after a heavy Indian meal. It is very popular at the Star of India.

| | |
|---|---|
| *1.2 litres (2 pints)* | **whole milk** |
| *425 ml (14 fl oz)* | **evaporated milk** |
| *115 g (4 oz)* | **sugar, or according to taste** |
| *1 x 267 g* | **can lychees** *finely chopped and drained* |
| *1–2 tbsp* | **ground almonds** |
| *1/2 tsp* | **ground cardamom** |

**serves 6–8**   Pour the milk into a large, heavy-bottomed saucepan and bring to the boil. Continue to boil for about 30 minutes, adjusting the heat to prevent it boiling over, and occasionally stirring to ensure that it does not stick to the base, then add the evaporated milk. As the milk thickens, stir continuously to prevent it sticking to the pan. Once the consistency is thick enough to coat the back of a spoon, remove from the heat.

Gradually add the sugar, a little at a time, stirring briskly to ensure the consistency remains smooth. Now put the pan back on the hob on a medium-to-low heat, and cook the mixture until it thickens and the sugar dissolves. As soon as the milk becomes the consistency of thick soup, remove from the heat and set aside to cool.

Once the mixture has cooled, add the lychees and whisk until they are evenly combined, then add the almonds and cardamom. Pour the mixture either into moulds or a plastic ice cream container and place in the top section of your freezer for about an hour until semi-set. Remove from the freezer and whisk with a fork in the moulds/container. Make sure that the consistency is smooth, then return the moulds to the freezer and allow the kulfi to set.

# sweet pancakes

Why not try this nutty pancake as a delicious, yet nutritious, alternative on Shrove Tuesday, or any other day, for that matter?

| | |
|---|---|
| 100 ml (3 1/2 fl oz) | **milk** |
| 375 ml (12 fl oz) | **coconut milk** |
| 1/2 tsp | **ground cardamom** |
| small pinch | **saffron strands** |
| 1/2 tsp | **ground nutmeg** |
| 50 g (2 oz) | **caster sugar** |
| 150 g (5 1/2 oz) | **plain flour** *sifted* |
| 100 g (3 1/2 oz) | **rice flour** *sifted* |
| 3 medium | **eggs** *beaten* |
| 200 ml (7 fl oz) | **vegetable oil or ghee** |

**for the pancake filling**

| | |
|---|---|
| 50 g (2 oz) | **white poppy seeds** |
| 100 g (3 1/2 oz) | **blanched almonds** *slivered* |
| 100 g (3 1/2 oz) | **pistachios** *slivered* |
| 150 g (5 1/2 oz) | **sultanas** |
| | **maple syrup/runny honey to drizzle** |

**serves 6–8** In a measuring jug, mix the milk, coconut milk, cardamom, saffron, nutmeg and sugar and then set aside. Put the flours in a large bowl, make a well in the centre and pour in the eggs. Gradually incorporate the eggs into the flour with a whisk, until you have absorbed most of the liquid. It will be quite dry at this stage so gradually add the milk mixture, whisking all the while. You should end up with a smooth batter that can drip from a spoon.

Combine the ingredients for the filling in a bowl. Heat a teaspoon of the oil in a frying pan and keep on a low-to-medium heat. Add one ladle (roughly a third of a cup) of batter to cover the base of the pan. Quickly add the filling – about one dessertspoon per pancake – before the batter starts to dry.

As the pancake cooks and bubbles at the edges, get ready to flip it over. Cook for 1 minute or so on the other side, then remove the pancake from the pan and place it on a plate. Continue until you have finished all the mixture.

To serve, fold each pancake into four, scatter over any remaining filling ingredients to decorate and drizzle with a tablespoon of runny honey or maple syrup.

# crunchy semolina biscuits *(Nankhetaye)*

These biscuits have a sensational, melt-in-the-mouth texture, and are delicious dunked into tea, hot chocolate or coffee. Stored in an airtight container or tin, they will keep for up to a month — if you manage not to consume them within the first day or so. Beware, they are very moreish and exceedingly rich. Strong men have been known to turn faint after consuming four.

| | |
|---|---|
| 175 g (6 oz) | **ghee** *melted* |
| 115 g (4 oz) | **caster sugar** |
| 2 small | **egg yolks** |
| $^1/_2$ tsp | **baking powder** |
| $^1/_4$ tsp | **ground cardamom** |
| $^1/_2$ tsp | **ground nutmeg** |
| pinch | **saffron strands** |
| 40 g (1 $^1/_2$ oz) | **semolina** |
| 225 g (8 oz) | **plain flour** |
| | **ground pistachios or ground almonds** *to garnish* |

**makes 12–16**     Combine the ghee and sugar in a bowl, whisking vigorously until the texture is smooth and creamy and the sugar has dissolved. Beat in the egg yolks, then add the baking powder, cardamom, nutmeg and saffron, and bind well. Gradually stir in the semolina and flour, then use an electric beater to bind everything together. This will take about 5 minutes. Cover and leave the dough to rest for about half an hour.

Preheat the oven to 200°C/400°F, Gas Mark 6. Form the dough into round balls about the size of a large walnut, and make an indent in the centre of each with your thumb. Place the biscuits on a greased baking sheet and bake in the oven for about 10–12 minutes. Avoid browning the biscuits, they should remain pale. Remove from the oven, sprinkle with ground pistachios or almonds, then allow to cool completely.

Teatime at The Troubadour.